BASIC/NOT BORING
MATH SKILLS

MIDDLE GRADE
BOOK OF
MATH TESTS

Series Concept & Development
by Imogene Forte & Marjorie Frank

Illustrations by Kathleen Bullock

Incentive Publications, Inc.
Nashville, Tennessee

About the cover:
Bound resist, or tie dye, is the most ancient known method of fabric surface design. The brilliance of the basic tie dye design on this cover reflects the possibilities that emerge from the mastery of basic skills.

Cover art by Mary Patricia Deprez, dba Tye Dye Mary®
Cover design by Marta Drayton and Joe Shibley
Edited by Angela Reiner

ISBN 0-86530-482-3

PRINTED IN THE UNITED STATES OF AMERICA
www.incentivepublications.com

TABLE OF CONTENTS

INSIDE THE
MIDDLE GRADE BOOK OF MATH TESTS

"I wish I had a convenient, fast way to assess basic skills and standards."

"If only I had a way to find out what my students already know about math!"

"If only I had a good way to find out what my students have learned!"

"How can I tell if my students are ready for state assessments?"

"It takes too long to create my own tests on the units I teach."

"The tests that come with my textbooks are too long and too dull."

"I need tests that cover all the skills on a topic—not just a few here and there."

This is what teachers tell us about their needs for testing materials. If you, too, are looking for quality, convenient materials that will help you gauge how well students are moving along towards mastering basic skills and standards—look no further. This is a book of tests such as you've never seen before! It's everything you've wanted in a group of ready-made math assessments for middle grade students.

- The tests are student-friendly. One glance through the book and you will see why. Students will be surprised that it's a test at all! These are like no other tests your students have seen before. One glance through the book will tell you that. The pages are inviting and fun. A clever rat, a feisty dog, and their friends tumble over the pages, leading students through math challenges and problems. Your students will not groan when you pass out these tests. They'll want to stick with them all the way to the end to see what's happening with the STOP sign this time!

- The tests are serious. Do not be fooled by the catchy characters and visual appeal. These are serious, thorough assessments of basic content. As a part of the BASIC/Not Boring Skills Series, they give broad coverage of skills with a flair that makes them favorites of teachers and kids.

- The tests cover all the basic skill areas for math. There are 22 tests within 6 areas: numbers & computation; fractions & decimals; problem solving; geometry & measurement; graphing, statistics, & probability; and pre-algebra.

- The tests are ready to use. In convenient and manageable sizes of 4, 6, 8, or 10 pages in length, each test covers a skill area (such as problem-solving strategies, plane geometry, or statistics & graphs) that should be assessed. Just give the pages to an individual student, or make copies for the entire class. Answer keys (included in back) are easy to find and easy to use.

- Skills are clearly identified. You can see exactly which skills are tested by reviewing the list of skills provided with each category of tests.

HOW TO USE THE
MIDDLE GRADE BOOK OF MATH TESTS

Each test can be used in many different ways. Here are a few:

- as a pre-test to see what a student knows or can do on a certain math topic
- as a post-test to find out how well students have mastered a content or skill area
- as a review to check up on student mastery of standards or readiness for state assessments
- as a survey to provide direction for your present or future instruction
- as an instructional tool to guide students through a review of a lesson
- with one student in an assessment or tutorial setting
- with a small group of students for assessment or instruction
- with a whole class for end-of-unit assessment

The book provides you with tools for using the tests effectively and keeping track of how students are progressing on skills or standards:

- 22 Tests on the Topics You Need: These are grouped according to broad topics within math. Each large grouping has three or more sub-tests. Tests are clearly labeled with subject area and specific topic.

- Skills Checklists Correlated to Test Items: At the beginning of each group of tests, you'll find a list of the skills covered. (For instance, pages 10 and 11 hold lists of skills for the four tests on numbers and computation.) Each skill is matched with the exact test items assessing that skill. If a student misses an item on the test, you'll know exactly which skill needs sharpening.

- Student Progress Records: Page 154 holds a reproducible form that can be used to track individual student achievement on all the tests in this book. Make a copy of this form for each student, and record the student's test scores and areas of instructional need.

- Class Progress Records: Pages 155–157 hold reproducible forms for keeping track of a whole class. You can record the dates that tests are given, and keep comments about what you learned from that test as well as notes for further instructional needs.

- Reference for Skill Sharpening Activities: Pages 158–159 describe a program of appealing exercises designed to teach, strengthen, or reinforce basic math skills and content. The skills covered in these books are correlated to national curriculum standards and the standards for many states.

- Scoring Guide for Performance Test: A performance test is given for math problem solving. For a complete scoring guide that assesses student performance on this test, see page 168.

- Answer Keys: An easy-to-use answer key is provided for each of the 22 tests. (See pages 162–174.)

THE MIDDLE GRADE MATH TESTS

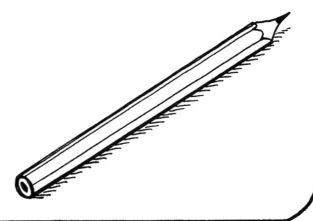

Numbers & Computation Skills Checklists

Numbers & Computation Test #1:

WHOLE NUMBER CONCEPTS

Test Location: pages 12–17

Skill	*Test Items*
Read and write whole numbers	1–6
Recognize or write numerals with their word names	1–6
Translate number words into numerals	5, 6
Identify a number in its expanded notation	7, 8
Compare and order whole numbers	9–12
Recognize prime and composite numbers	13
Identify place value of whole numbers	14–18
Round whole numbers	19–23
Recognize a number in a variety of equivalent forms	24, 25
Identify multiples and common multiples	26, 27
Identify factors of a number	28
Identify common factors and greatest common factors	29–32
Analyze and extend patterns and sequences	33–36
Compare large numbers using symbols <, >, and =	37–44
Estimate numbers and amounts	45–50

Numbers & Computation Test #2:

ADDITION & SUBTRACTION

Test Location: pages 18–21

Skill	*Test Items*
Estimate sums or differences	1, 6, 21
Use information from a table to solve addition and subtraction problems	1–6
Compute addition and subtraction problems	7, 8
Check the accuracy of addition or subtraction computation	9, 13
Find a number that meets specifications described in a word problem	10–12
Analyze and extend number patters that involve addition or subtraction	14, 15
Solve equations with addition or subtraction	16
Use mental math to solve addition and subtraction problems	17–21
Solve word problems with addition and subtraction	22–25

Middle Grade Book of Math Tests

Numbers & Computation Test #3:

MULTIPLICATION & DIVISION

Test Location: pages 22–25

Skill	*Test Items*
Solve word problems with multiplication and division	1, 2
Use multiplication or division find a missing number	3, 4
Compute multiplication and division problems	5, 6
Analyze and extend number patterns involving multiplication or division	7, 8
Verify answers to multiplication or division problems	9, 10
Find averages	11, 28
Check the accuracy of a multiplication or division solution	12
Multiply with multiples of 10	13–17
Divide with multiplies of 10	18–22
Identify the value of exponential numbers	23
Solve equations with addition or subtraction	24
Estimate solutions to multiplication or division problems	25–27
Solve word problems with multiplication or division	28–30

Numbers & Computation Test #4:

MIXED OPERATIONS

Test Location: pages 26–31

Skill	*Test Items*
Choose the correct operation to solve a one-step problem	1–3, 6–9
Choose the correct operations to solve multi-step problems	4, 5
Identify the order of operations in multi-step problems	4, 5, 10–12
Estimate answers to problems using a variety of operations	13, 14
Compute answers using addition, subtraction, multiplication, or division	15, 16
Use one of the four operations to find missing numbers	17–19
Use an opposite operation to verify the solution to a computation	20, 21
Use various operations to solve word problems	22, 23, 38–40
Identify properties of operations and their uses	24–30
Find averages	31–33, 40
Solve equations with various operations	34, 35
Identify the value of exponential numbers	36, 37
Check the accuracy of a solution	38

Middle Grade Book of Math Tests

WHOLE NUMBER CONCEPTS

Name _____

Possible Correct Answers: 50

Date _____

Your Correct Answers: _____

406,319,003

1. Spike is proudly showing off his favorite large number.
What is the accurate way to read this numeral?

　a. four hundred sixty million, three hundred thousand nineteen, three
　b. four hundred sixty million, three hundred nineteen thousand, three
　c. four hundred six million, three hundred nineteen thousand, three
　d. four hundred six million, three hundred nineteen thousand, thirty

2. Write this numeral in words.

154,880 _____

3. Write this numeral in words.

111,008 _____

4. Write this numeral in words.

77,050,050 _____

5. Write the numeral.

sixty-five million, four hundred thousand, ten _____

6. Write the numeral.

two hundred eighty thousand, one hundred four _____

7. Which number is the same as 313,960?

    a. 300,000 + 10,000 + 3000 + 900 + 6   c. 300,000 + 10,000 + 3000 + 900 + 6

    b. 30,00 + 1000 + 300 + 96   d. 300,000 + 10,000 + 3000 + 900 + 60

---

8. Which number is the same as 808,000,080?

    a. 800,000 + 8,000 + 80   c. 800,000,000 + 8000 + 80

    b. 800,000,000 + 8,000,000 + 80   d. 8,000,000,000 + 8,000,000 + 8

---

9. Circle the least number.

    803,460   803,450   830,640   844,604

10. Circle the **greatest number** on Leroy's shirt.

11. Circle the **least number** on Spike's shirt.

12. Write these in order from smallest to largest:

    256,369   265,396   256,938   265,398

    _____   _____   _____   _____

13. Circle the prime numbers on this measuring stick.

Name _____

Middle Grade Book of Math Tests

14. What is the place value of the **8** in this number?

908, 960, 113 _____

15. What is the place value of the **5** in this number?

405,870 _____

16. What number is in the **ten thousands** place?

721,804,303 _____

17. What number is in the **hundred thousands** place?

663, 409, 601 _____

18. What number is in the **ten millions** place?

301,182,755 _____

19. Round this number **to the nearest hundred:**

55, 876 _____

20. Round this number to the nearest **thousand:**

3,624,730 _____

21. Round this number to the nearest **ten thousand:**

692,504 _____

22. Round this number to the nearest **ten million:**

62,999,909 _____

23. Spike is showing off the number of miles he's covered on his skateboard. Round this number to the nearest **hundred**.

Answer _____

Name _____

Middle Grade Book of Math Tests

24. Circle the number on the sign that does NOT have the same value as the other numbers.

Forty thousand, four hundred four
40,000 + 4000 + 400 + 4
40,404
4 ten thousands, 4 hundreds, 4 ones
Twice 20,202

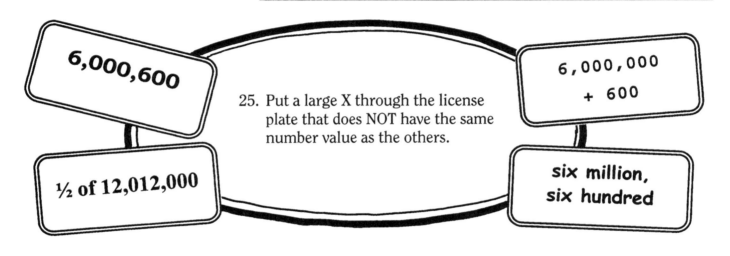

6,000,600

½ of 12,012,000

25. Put a large X through the license plate that does NOT have the same number value as the others.

6,000,000 + 600

six million, six hundred

26. Circle the multiples of 7.

14   24   35   54   28   56   70

27. Circle the common multiples of 4 and 6.

12   16   8   20   24   48

28. Write the factors of 18. _____

29. Write the common factors of 12 and 64. _____

30. Write the common factors of 9 and 24. _____

31. What is the greatest common factor of 30 and 48? _____

32. What is the greatest common factor of 66 and 88? _____

Middle Grade Book of Math Tests

33. Write the missing numbers to fit the pattern.

1   3   6   10   ☐   21   28   36   ☐

34. Write the missing numbers to fit the pattern.

9812   8723   ☐   6545   ☐   4367   3278

35. Write the missing numbers to finish the pattern.

10,500   10,400   9,400   9,300   8,300   ☐   ☐

36. Finish the pattern on the flags.

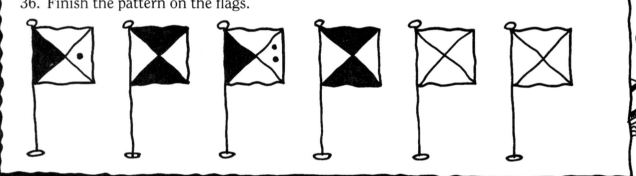

In 37–44, fill in the blanks with **<**, **>**, or **=**.

37.   154,869,471 ☐ 154,896,417   41.   88,080,808 ☐ 88,088,080

38.   1,600,000 ☐ 610,000   42.   9000 x 800 ☐ 120 x 60,000

39.   30,033,330 ☐ 30,033,030   43.   10 x 100,000 ☐ 100 x 1000

40.   27,000 ☐ 270,000   44.   200 x 70 ☐ 1400 x 100

Name _____

45. During the **57** skateboard competitions, the Western Division Team recorded **6,304** bruises and other minor injuries.
The Eastern Division Team suffered **4,697** minor injuries.
Which describes the amount of combined injuries?

      a. about 10,000   c. about 11,000

      b. about 3,000   d. about 12,000

46. Which number is closest to seven hundred twenty thousand?

    a. 71,999   b. 7,246,700   c. 707, 398   d. 717,555

ATTENDANCE AT SKATEBOARD COMPETITIONS	
CITY	Number of Spectators
Albuquerque	15,615
Phoenix	8,988
Salt Lake City	13,705
Des Moines	6,977
Tallahassee	9,112

47. Which city had about 100 more spectators than Phoenix had?

    _____

48. Which city had a number of spectators that is more than twice the number in Des Moines?

    _____

49. Spike's travel cost $852. Whose travel cost about $75 less than his?

    a. Leroy's travel—$777

        b. Chichi's travel—$926

            c. Buster's travel—$790

               d. Duke's travel—$801

50. Which two friends together have practiced about 5000 hours?

    a. Chichi—2860 hours

    b. Duke—1967 hours

    c. Leroy—3100 hours

    d. Spike—1509 hours

    _____ and

    _____

Middle Grade Book of Math Tests

ADDITION & SUBTRACTION

Name _____   Possible Correct Answers: 25

Date _____   Your Correct Answers: _____

Do not use a calculator for any part of this test.

MEDAL WINNERS

Runner	Number of Medals
Rhoda	61
Nellie	48
Cass	33
Roxie	44
Lucinda	16
Chichi	25
Mimi	55

Use this chart to solve problems 1–6.

1. Estimate the total number of medals:
   a. about 310
   b. about 250
   c. about 350
   d. about 280

2. How many more medals has Rhoda won than anybody else?

   _____

3. Who has won 19 fewer medals than Roxie?

   _____

4. What is the total number of medals
   won by the four runners with the most medals? _____

5. How many more medals has Cass won than Lucinda? _____

6. Who has won approximately 30 fewer medals than Nellie?

   _____

18

7. Compute:

601,855,199
+   32,189,936

8. Which answer is correct?

661,001
−   98,294

a. 759,295   c. 673,817

b. 562,707   d. 662,707

9. Write an addition problem to check the accuracy of Spike's answer.

Is it correct? (Circle yes or no.)

Yes, or No?

38,096
−14,299
23,805

compute here:

10. A certain number, when subtracted from 24,005, yields an answer of 15,005. What is the number?

_____

11. A number, when added to 75,006,006, yields 80,000,000. What is the number?

_____

12. Leroy's racing number is the difference between 11,023 and 10,090. What is it?

_____

Name _____   **19**   _____

13. Chichi adds up the number of miles she's run in the last 6 months. Did she get the right answer? Circle yes or no.

yes   no

```
Jan   116
Feb   209
Mar    82
Apr   151
May    99
June  130
      ___
      787
```

14. Find the pattern. Write the missing numbers.

7   18   29   40   51   ☐ ☐ ☐

15. Find the pattern. Write the missing numbers.

1000   990   970   ☐   900   850   ☐ ☐

16. Both of these equations have the same solution for **x**.
What is **x**?

$195 - x = 38$ $x + 46 = 203$

x = ☐   x = ☐

Solve:

17. $50{,}000 - 4{,}000 + 40 - 1{,}200 =$

_____

18. $27{,}000{,}100 + 50{,}000 - 7{,}000{,}000 =$

_____

19. $9{,}999 - 5{,}555 + 444 - 4{,}000 =$

_____

20. $123{,}456 - 456 + 123{,}456 =$

_____

21. Which problem has an answer of more than 4500?
    a. 18,369 – 13,669
    b. 14,000 + 2,370 – 15,005
    c. 150,050 + 75 – 148,100 + 20
    d. 900 + 1300 + 1700 – 590

22. A pole-vaulter practiced her sport for 284 hours during the season. A hurdler practiced 57 hours more than the pole-vaulter. During the same period of time, a long distance runner ran 15 hours more than both the others combined. How many hours did the runner spend running?

    Answer: _____

23. The track team went on a shopping trip at the beginning of the season. They spent $785 on track shoes, $98 on socks, and $365 on running shorts. On the way home, they ate dinner for $46.50. They began with a check worth $2000. How much money was left over?

    Answer: _____

24. At the track meet, the teams from Oregon won a total of 218 medals. (This includes gold, silver, and bronze.) 73 medals were gold. 52 were bronze. How many medals were silver?

    Answer: _____

25. Spike is buying Energy Drink and Energy Bars for the team. The drink will cost $79.50. The Energy Bars will cost $15.75. No tax will be charged. He takes $100 bill to the store. Will this be enough money?

    yes   no

MULTIPLICATION & DIVISION

Name _____

Possible Correct Answers: 30

Date _____

Your Correct Answers: _____

Do not use a calculator for any part of this test.

1. The stadium at the track has a total of **54,450** seats. The seats are divided into **90** sections.
How many seats are in each section?

Answer_____

2. Fans paid **$25,248** to watch last week's race. The tickets cost **$8.00** each.
How many fans watched the race?

Answer_____

3. A number, when divided by 35, yields an answer of 665.

What is the number? _____

4. A number, when multiplied by 99, yields a product of 10,890.

What is the number? _____

Compute.

5.
$$68,033$$
$$x \quad 56$$

6.
$$7,560 \div 36 =$$

7. Find the division pattern. Write the missing numbers.

100,000   20,000   4,000   800   ☐   ☐

8. Find the multiplication pattern. Write the missing numbers.

16   48   144   ☐   1296   ☐   ☐

9. Which answer is correct?

$$\begin{array}{r} 4,109 \\ \times\ 456 \\ \hline \end{array}$$

a. 1,873,704   c. 873,704

b. 1,860,604   d. 1,873,654

10. Which answer is correct?

$$555 \div 37 =$$

a. 25   c. 16 R 6

b. 15   d. 14

11. A high jumper practiced for 46 hours last week.
In that time, he completed 598 practice jumps.
On the average, how many jumps did he try each hour?

Answer: _____

Middle Grade Book of Math Tests

12. Leroy was in charge of providing water for the thirsty runners. There were 233 runners entered in the race. He was told that each runner would drink approximately 7 quarts of water during each day. Leroy calculated the amount of water he would need to provide for the 2-day event. Did he get it right?
(Circle yes or no.)

yes   no

$$\begin{array}{r} \overset{2\ 2}{2\,3\,3} \\ \times\ 7 \\ \hline 1\,6\,3\,1 \end{array}$$
quarts

Find the missing numbers.

13. **20 x 800 =** ⬚

14. **36 x** ⬚ **= 7200**

15. ⬚ **x 6000 = 30,000,000**

16. **250 x 400 =** ⬚

17. **120 x** ⬚ **= 60,000**

18. **45,000 ÷** ⬚ **= 500**

19. ⬚ **÷ 800 = 90**

20. **28,000 ÷ 700 =** ⬚

21. **320,000 ÷** ⬚ **= 8**

22. ⬚ **÷ 11 = 2000**

23. Which has a value of 1,000,000?

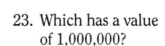

a. 10^2 d. 10^5
b. 10^3 e. 10^6
c. 10^4 f. 10^7

24. Solve the equation for x.

$$x + 10 = 10,300$$
$$x = \underline{\hspace{2cm}}$$

25. Estimate to tell which problem has an answer of more than 4500.
   a. (790 x 13) ÷ 4
   b. 400,000 ÷ (5100 x 12)
   c. (290 ÷ 5) x 81
   d. (815 x 32) ÷ 12,000

26. 28 athletes traveled 48 miles each to the track meet. 150 athletes traveled 89 miles. Estimate the number of miles traveled by all the athletes.

   Estimated answer: _____

27. The booster club sold hot dogs at 18 track meets. They sold a total of 5310. Approximately how many hot dogs did they sell at each meet?

   Estimated answer: _____

28. 190 runners used 570 gallons of water taking showers after the track meet. On the average, how much water did each runner use?

   Answer: _____

29. A school uses 3 dozen bars of shower soap each week for the 14-week track season. The total spent on soap is $151.20. What is the cost of each bar of soap?

   Answer: _____

30. Each of the 37 track team members uses 2 towels for the after-practice shower. The team practices 5 times a week during a 15-week season. How many towels are used during the season?

   Answer: _____

Name _____

25

MIXED OPERATIONS

Name _____   Possible Correct Answers: 40

Date _____   Your Correct Answers: _____

Do not use a calculator for any part of this test.

---

1. Spike took about **45** nasty spills a week while practicing new skating tricks.
   To find out how many spills he took in ten weeks, you would

   add
   subtract
   multiply
   divide

2. **96** skaters in a race drank **672** quarts of *Energy Juice* during a race.
   To find out how much each skater drank, you would

   add
   subtract
   multiply
   divide

3. A skater was rushed to the hospital about once every **14** minutes during the $6\frac{1}{2}$ hour race. To find the number of ambulance trips during the race, you would

   add
   subtract
   multiply
   divide

4. 160 skaters pre-registered for the race. 32 did not show up to start the race. Another 47 registered at the start of the race. To find out how many skaters started the race, you would
   a. add, then subtract
   b. add, then add again
   c. subtract, then add
   d. subtract, then subtract again

5. 66 skaters entered a race. Each skater paid a $25 entrance fee. The race committee spent $400 on T-shirts, drinks, and food for the skaters. The rest of the money was donated to a charity. To find out how much was donated to charity, you would
   a. add, then multiply
   b. multiply, then add
   c. divide, then subtract
   d. multiply, then subtract

Fill in the missing sign for each problem.

6. **28,000** ☐ **140 = 200**

8. **500** ☐ **60 = 30,000**

7. **8963** ☐ **255 = 8708**

9. **69,500** ☐ **1500 = 71,000**

10. If you were asked to compute this, what would you do first?

$$(160 + 17) \times 6 - 89 =$$

a. multiply

b. subtract

c. add

d. It doesn't matter. The answer is the same any way you compute it.

11. If you were asked to compute this, what would you do first?

$$10,000 - (36 \times 3) + 12 =$$

a. multiply

b. subtract

c. add

d. It doesn't matter. The answer is the same any way you compute it.

12. Leroy is trying to work out his practice schedule for the next 7 days. On most days, he has 4 hours free to practice. However, on Monday he needs one of those hours for a doctor's appointment. On Thursday, he needs 2 of those hours to study for a test. On Sunday, he can practice for 3 extra hours.

What operation should he do first to solve his problem?

a. multiply

b. subtract

c. add

d. It doesn't matter. The answer is the same any way you compute it.

Middle Grade Book of Math Tests

13. Three skaters brag about the number of miles they've covered in skating practice this month. Spike has skated 187 miles. Chichi has skated twice that many miles. Ginger has covered 211 miles. About how many miles total have the three skated?

Answer: _____

14. Which answer is about 750?

a. 68 x 15 + 100   b. (888 ÷ 6) x 5   c. (9,221 – 1200) ÷ 40   d. 36 x 71

15. Solve.

$$100,000 - 45,000 + 505 =$$

_____

16. Solve.

$$(66,666 + 1234 - 120) \div 2 =$$

_____

17. Chichi's race number is the difference between the product of 83 and 12 and the product of 16 and 9.

Write Chichi's number on her shirt.

18. What number is 10,001 less than the product of 140 and 3000?

19. What number is 550 times the difference between 8600 and 7600?

Name _____

Middle Grade Book of Math Tests

20. Use another operation to verify the answer to this problem.

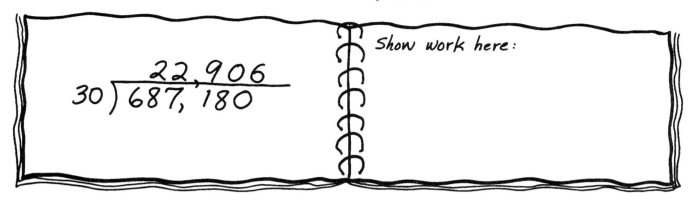

Show work here:

$$30\overline{)687,180}\quad 22,906$$

21. Use another operation to verify the answer to this problem.

Show work here:

$$\begin{array}{r} 627 \\ \times\ 85 \\ \hline 53,295 \end{array}$$

22. 378 skaters entered the 1999 Hot Wheels Skating Competition. In 1995, when the event began, 49 skaters took part. In both years, more than half the skaters were under age 18.

Given this information, which statement below is NOT necessarily true?

    a. The number of skaters in 1999 was about eight times the number in 1995.

    b. In 1999, over 200 skaters were under age 18.

    c. At least 214 skaters total (in 1995 and 1999) were under 18.

    d. The 1995 event had 329 fewer skaters than the 1999 event.

23. The 400 skaters in the Hot Wheels 2000 Competition came to the race with about $120,000 worth of clothing and equipment. Skaters spent about $80,000 in travel and lodging costs. In addition, each skater paid a $60 entrance fee to compete.

Given this information, which statement below is NOT necessarily true?

    a. Skaters spent a total of $24,000 on entrance fees.

    b. The skaters' expenses described totaled $200,600.

    c. On the average, each skater spent about $560 on the expenses described.

    d. The average skater spent $260 on travel, lodging, and entrance fees.

Name _____ **29** _____

Write the letter that shows the property demonstrated in each equation.

A = Associative Property   **C** = Commutative Property

D = Distributive Property   **I** = Identity Property

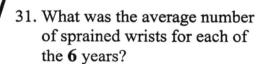

Ouch!

____ 24. **28 + (100 − x) = (28 + 100) − x**

____ 25. **85,609 x 1 = 85,609**

____ 26. **(15,000 x 7) x 2 = 15,000 x (7 x 2)**

____ 27. **100(36 − 5) = 100 x 36 − 100 x 5**

____ 28. **17 + 90 + 30 + 4 = 90 + 4 + 30 + 17**

____ 29. **59 x 75 + 59 x 60 = 59 (75 + 60)**

____ 30. **36,000 x 4 = 4 x 36,000**

SKATERS' INJURIES						
Injury	1995	1996	1997	1998	1999	2000
Broken Noses	14	9	20	11	6	0
Sprained Wrists	31	17	22	28	40	18
Serious Scrapes & Bruises	20	22	36	13	44	15
Broken Wrists or Arms	7	3	9	19	10	6
Broken Legs	6	0	5	6	9	4
Split Lips	21	9	0	12	6	0

31. What was the average number of sprained wrists for each of the **6** years?

_____

32. What was the average number of broken bones (legs, wrists, or arms) for each of the **6** years?

_____

33. Which injury had the highest average frequency over the **6-year** period?

_____

34. Which is the correct value for x?

$$950 - x + 16{,}000 = 16{,}666$$

    a. x = 1516   b. x = 15,050   c. x = 284

35. Which is the correct value for y?

$$10{,}000 \times 10 + y - 10{,}000 = 100{,}000$$

    a. y = 1000   b. y = 10,000   c. y = 100,000

36. Which is the value of 10^5?

    a. 10,000

    b. 10,000,000

    c. 1,000,000

    d. 100,000

37. Which is the value of 14^3?

    a. 196

    b. 2744

    c. 784

    d. 38, 414

38. Spike claims he has skated 720 miles this month. His friend Chichi has skated 86 miles less. Leroy has skated 38 miles more than Chichi. Butch has skated 150 miles more than Leroy.

Spike wants to figure out who has skated the most miles. He is confident that he is the one with the most miles. Check his math. Is he right?

        Yes   No

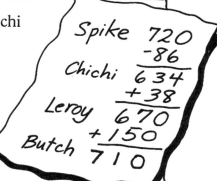

Spike 720
−86
Chichi 634
+38
Leroy 670
+150
Butch 710

39. 285 skaters share 57 pizzas. How many skaters will each pizza have to feed?

Answer: _____

40. During the year, the Lucky County Skaters have traveled 5120 miles to skating competitions. They have taken part in 32 competitions. On the average, how far did they travel on each trip?

Answer: _____

Name _____

Middle Grade Book of Math Tests

Fractions & Decimals Skills Checklists

Fractions & Decimals Test #1:

FRACTIONS

Test Location: pages 34–41

Skill	Test Items
Write numeral and word names of fractions	1–9
Use fractions to describe part of a group	10–16
Compare fractions and order fractions	17–20
Identify and write fractions in lowest terms	21–26
Identify and write equivalent fractions	27–29
Write fractions as mixed numerals and mixed numerals as fractions	30–35
Add and subtract fractions with like denominators	36, 37
Add and subtract fractions with unlike denominators	38–40
Solve word problems with fractions	38, 43, 48, 53–57, 62–65
Verify or check accuracy of answers to fraction problems	38, 41, 42, 44
Perform operations with mixed numerals	41, 42, 44, 48, 49–51
Multiply Fractions	43–45, 47, 48
Divide Fractions	46, 47, 50
Solve equations with fractions	51, 52
Solve problems with ratio	53–55
Solve proportion problems	56–61
Solve rate-time-distance problems	62–65

Fractions & Decimals Test #2:

DECIMALS

Test Location: pages 42–47

Skill	Test Items
Read and write decimal numerals and word names	1–12
Identify place value in decimals	13–16
Compare and order decimals	17, 18
Round decimals	19–22
Add and subtract decimals	23, 25–28
Multiply and divide decimals	24, 29–40
Solve word problems with decimals	24, 25, 28, 38, 47, 50
Verify or check answers to decimal problems	29, 31–36, 38
Solve equations with decimals	39, 40
Change decimals to percents	41–46
Solve word problems with percents	48–50

Fractions & Decimals Test #3:

FRACTIONS, DECIMALS, & PERCENTS

Test Location: pages 48–51

Skill	*Test Items*
Write fractions as decimals	1–3, 32, 35, 39
Write decimals as fractions	4–6, 33, 36, 37
Write percents as decimals	7–12, 17–22, 34, 38
Write decimals as percents	13–16, 33, 36, 37
Find a percentage of a number	17–24, 27
Solve problems that involve finding percent	23, 24, 31, 40–45
Given a calculated percentage, find the original number	25, 26
Verify or check the accuracy of problems involving fractions, decimals, and/or percents	28
Write fractions as percents	28, 29, 32, 35, 39
Write percents as fractions	30, 34, 38
Recognize and write the fraction, decimal, and percent that represent a value	32–39

Fractions & Decimals Test #4:

MONEY

Test Location: pages 52–55

Skill	*Test Items*
Identify the value of different combinations of money bills	1–8
Add and subtract amounts of money	9, 10
Solve word problems that involve money	11, 12, 18, 22–25
Multiply and divide amounts of money	11–16
Verify and/or check accuracy of money problems	15, 16, 21
Find averages of money amounts	17, 18
Write and solve equations involving money	19, 20
Solve money problems involving interest	19

FRACTIONS

Name _____

Possible Correct Answers: 65

Date _____

Your Correct Answers: _____

Do not use a calculator for any part of this test.

1. Write a numeral to match these words. **five twelfths** _____

2. Write a numeral to match these words.
   sixty-seven and three fifths _____

3. Write a numeral to match these words.
   twelve and eight ninths _____

4. Write a numeral to match these words.
   eighty-six and eight fifteenths _____

5. Write a numeral to match these words.
   eleven and four-fifths _____

Write the name of each number in words.

6. $\dfrac{9}{11}$: _____

7. $20\dfrac{3}{4}$: _____

8. $1000\dfrac{1}{2}$: _____

9. $\dfrac{7}{12}$: _____

Write a fraction for each answer.

10. What fraction of the swimmers is shown with a towel? _____

11. What fraction of the swimmers does NOT have a snorkel? _____

12. What fraction of the feet has flippers? _____

13. What fraction of the swimmers has goggles? _____

14. What fraction of the swimmers has a suit with stripes? _____

15. What fraction of the swimmers with striped suits has a snorkel? _____

16. What fraction of the swimmers with goggles has flippers? _____

17. Circle the largest fraction.

$\frac{1}{2}$ $\frac{3}{4}$ $\frac{7}{8}$ $\frac{3}{5}$ $\frac{1}{12}$ $\frac{2}{7}$

18. Circle the smallest fraction.

$\frac{3}{8}$ $\frac{2}{3}$ $\frac{5}{6}$ $\frac{1}{15}$ $\frac{1}{2}$ $\frac{7}{10}$

Name _____

35

Middle Grade Book of Math Tests

19. Spike swam $\frac{3}{5}$ mile before breakfast. Sal swam $\frac{5}{8}$ mile before breakfast. Who swam farther?

Answer: _____

20. **Read the fractions on the balls. Write them in order from smallest to largest.**

_____

21. Circle the fractions that are in lowest terms.

$\frac{6}{11}$ $\frac{12}{15}$ $\frac{7}{21}$ $\frac{4}{5}$ $\frac{2}{3}$ $\frac{9}{13}$

22. Circle the fractions that are in lowest terms.

$\frac{5}{16}$ $\frac{2}{10}$ $\frac{28}{39}$ $\frac{5}{12}$ $\frac{11}{18}$

23. Write this fraction in lowest terms: $\frac{15}{20}$ _____	25. Write this fraction in lowest terms. $\frac{12}{15}$ _____
24. Write this fraction in lowest terms. $\frac{20}{32}$ _____	26. Write this fraction in lowest terms. $\frac{11}{44}$ _____

Middle Grade Book of Math Tests

27. A swimmer missed $\frac{1}{3}$ of the competition season with an injury.
Circle the fractions that are equivalent to this amount.

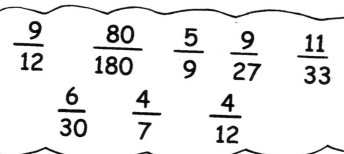

$$\frac{9}{12} \qquad \frac{80}{180} \qquad \frac{5}{9} \qquad \frac{9}{27} \qquad \frac{11}{33}$$

$$\frac{6}{30} \qquad \frac{4}{7} \qquad \frac{4}{12}$$

28. Circle the fractions that are equivalent to $\frac{6}{15}$. $\qquad \frac{1}{5} \qquad \frac{3}{5} \qquad \frac{9}{30} \qquad \frac{18}{45} \qquad \frac{2}{5} \qquad \frac{12}{30}$

29. Write three fractions that are equivalent to $\frac{3}{5}$.

30. While Chichi practiced her ocean swimming, a friend rowed beside her in a boat.

Her practice today lasted $2\frac{5}{6}$ hours. Which fraction shows this amount of time?

a. $\frac{25}{6}$ b. $\frac{15}{6}$ c. $\frac{17}{6}$ d. $\frac{16}{6}$

31. Chichi has been swimming competitively for $\frac{23}{5}$ years. Write this as a mixed numeral.

32. A series of swimming races has lasted $9\frac{6}{7}$ weeks. Write this as a fraction.

33. Write $\frac{48}{7}$ as a mixed numeral.

34. Write $\frac{113}{6}$ as a mixed numeral.

35. Write $20\frac{3}{4}$ as a fraction.

Middle Grade Book of Math Tests

36. Calculate:

$$\frac{5}{12} + \frac{3}{12} - \frac{1}{12} + \frac{4}{12} =$$

37. Calculate:

$$\frac{11}{9} - \frac{6}{9} + \frac{2}{9} =$$

38. The first race lasted $\frac{2}{3}$ of an hour.

The second race lasted $\frac{3}{10}$ of an hour.

Leroy calculated that the second game was $\frac{1}{3}$ hour

longer than the first. Is he right?

yes   no

39. Write the answer in lowest terms.

$$\frac{7}{12} + \frac{3}{4} =$$

40. Write the answer in lowest terms.

$$\frac{14}{20} - \frac{3}{12} =$$

41. Which answer is correct?

$$4\frac{1}{2} + 80\frac{3}{5} = \boxed{}$$

a. $85\frac{1}{10}$

b. 85

c. $82\frac{2}{5}$

d. $204\frac{1}{2}$

e. none of these

42. Which answer is correct?

$$20\frac{2}{3} - 12\frac{5}{6} = \boxed{}$$

a. $8\frac{3}{6}$

b. $7\frac{2}{3}$

c. $8\frac{3}{6}$

d. $33\frac{1}{2}$

e. none of these

Name

38

43. Rhoda saw **108** fish while she was swimming.

Cici saw $\frac{2}{3}$ as many fish as Rhoda.

How many fish did Cici see?

Answer: _____

A.

$$\frac{2}{7} \times \frac{5}{8} = \frac{2}{13}$$

B.

$$3\frac{1}{3} \times 2\frac{7}{10} = \frac{10}{27}$$

44. Which problems above (A and B) are correctly solved?

a. A only   b. B only   c. A and B   d. neither

45. Write the answer in lowest terms: $\frac{7}{9} \times \frac{5}{7}$ = _____

46. Write the answer in lowest terms: $\frac{12}{15} \div \frac{3}{4}$ = _____

47. The answer to a problem is $\frac{2}{3}$.
What is the problem?

a. $\frac{2}{3} \div \frac{1}{2}$ =

b. $\frac{5}{8} \times \frac{2}{3}$ =

c. $\frac{4}{9} \div \frac{4}{6}$ =

d. none of these

Name _____

Middle Grade Book of Math Tests

48. Pizza was delivered on the beach.

    When Spike arrived, there were $7\frac{1}{2}$ pizzas left.

    He ate $\frac{1}{5}$ of the pizza that was left.

    How much did he eat?

    Answer: _____

49. Write the answer in lowest terms.

    $$\frac{2}{11} + 12\frac{6}{11} - 3\frac{10}{11} =$$

    _____

50. Is the answer correct?

    $$12\frac{2}{4} \div 5\frac{1}{3} = 2\frac{11}{32}$$

    Yes   No

51. Solve for x.

    $x + 125\frac{1}{4} = 250\frac{3}{4}$

    $x =$ _____

52. Solve for y.

    $\frac{2}{3}y = 44$

    $y =$ _____

53. Spike entered 13 races last month. He won 7.
    Write a ratio to show the comparison of his losses
    to the total number of races he entered.

    Answer: _____

54. A team of swimmers drove 240 miles to a race.
    They used 16 gallons of gas on the trip.
    How many miles did they get per gallon?

    Answer: _____

55. Spike won a 5-mile race in 36 minutes.
    How many minutes did each mile take?

    Answer: _____

Name _____

Middle Grade Book of Math Tests

56. At the end of a long practice, Spike drank 4 quarts of water in 47 seconds. How much water did he drink per second?

Answer _____

57. One clever young rat earned money giving quick neck rubs before races. He could give neck rubs to 3 swimmers in one minute. Before one race, he gave neck rubs to 27 swimmers. How much time did this take him?

Answer _____

Find x to solve each proportion.

58. $\frac{x}{90} = \frac{3}{10}$

$x =$ _____

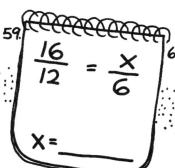

59. $\frac{16}{12} = \frac{x}{6}$

$x =$ _____

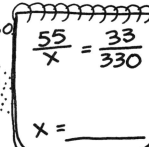

60. $\frac{55}{x} = \frac{33}{330}$

$x =$ _____

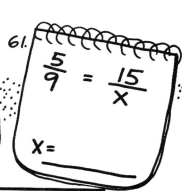

61. $\frac{5}{9} = \frac{15}{x}$

$x =$ _____

62. The cook who serves submarine sandwiches at the beach can make **30** sandwiches in **42** minutes. How long would it take him to make **10** sandwiches?

Answer_____

63. The scale on a map of an obstacle course for swimmers is **5 cm = 1000 m.** Two buoys are **12 cm** apart on the map. How far apart are they in reality?

Answer_____

64. Grover cleans up the beach with his new beach-sweeper. He can clean a **10-mile** stretch in **45** minutes. How long will it take him to clean the **28-mile** beach?

Answer_____

65. For every **50** swimmers who enter the ocean race, **8** drop out before the race is finished. If **12** dropped out, how many swimmers entered?

Answer_____

Middle Grade Book of Math Tests

DECIMALS

Name _____

Possible Correct Answers: 50

Date _____

Your Correct Answers: _____

Do not use a calculator for any part of this test.

Choose the numeral (from the flags) that matches the words.
Write the numeral.

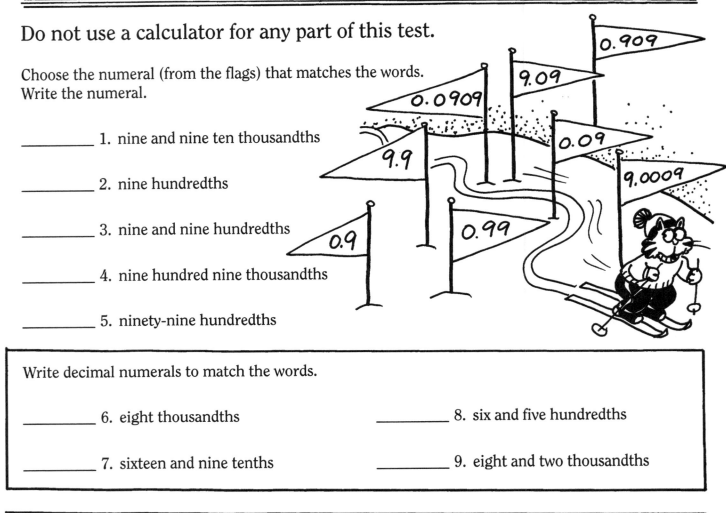

_____ 1. nine and nine ten thousandths

_____ 2. nine hundredths

_____ 3. nine and nine hundredths

_____ 4. nine hundred nine thousandths

_____ 5. ninety-nine hundredths

Write decimal numerals to match the words.

_____ 6. eight thousandths

_____ 7. sixteen and nine tenths

_____ 8. six and five hundredths

_____ 9. eight and two thousandths

Write each numeral in words.

10. 12.06 _____

11. 0.007 _____

12. 1.077 _____

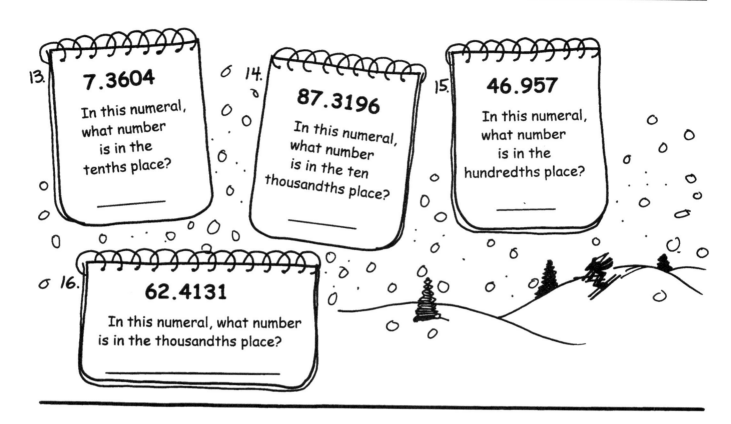

13. 7.3604

In this numeral, what number is in the tenths place?

_____

14. 87.3196

In this numeral, what number is in the ten thousandths place?

_____

15. 46.957

In this numeral, what number is in the hundredths place?

_____

16. 62.4131

In this numeral, what number is in the thousandths place?

_____

17. Write the names of the racers in the order of their finish, placing the fastest skier first.

Downhill Racing Times	
Skier	Fastest Time In Minutes
Sal	2.9118
Spike	3.0092
Bess	2.9109
Chichi	2.9504
Sly	2.9076
Leroy	2.9368

a. _____

b. _____

c. _____

d. _____

e. _____

f. _____

18. Which is the correct order of these numerals (from smallest to largest)?

a.   0.06,   7.707,   0.66,   0.67,   7.077

b.   7.077,   0.06,   0.66,   0.67,   7.707

c.   0.67,   7.707,   7.077,   0.06,   0.66

d.   0.06,   0.66,   0.67,   7.077,   7.707

Middle Grade Book of Math Tests

19. Round Leroy's number to the nearest tenth.

_____

20. Round Chichi's number to the nearest thousandth.

_____

21. Round Spike's number to the nearest hundredth.

_____

22. Round Bess's number to the nearest ten thousandth.

_____

23. Choose the correct answer.

   56.5 – 12.2 + 70.6 = _____

   a. 139.1   b. 114.9   c. 110.9   d. none of these

24. The ski team drank **16.2** quarts of hot chocolate. The team has **18** members. How much hot chocolate did the average player drink?

   Answer: _____

25. Spike skied **3.68** miles on Monday, **4.2** miles on Tuesday, and **2.88** miles on Wednesday. How far did he ski in these 3 days?

   Answer: _____

26. Compute:

1987.654

-93.708

27. Compute:

700.08 + 0.909 =

28. Speedy Sly got down the hill in 3 minutes and 54.083 seconds.
Sassy Sal's time was 3 minutes and 54.174 seconds.
Sam Shoosh made it to the finish line in 3 minutes and 45.069 seconds.

Who won the race? _____

How much faster was the winner
than the second place finisher? _____

29. Which problem is solved correctly?

a. **35.06 x .04 = 140.24**

b. **42.11 x .05 = 2.1055**

c. **700.07 x 1.02 = 1480.021**

d. **0.09 x 0.50 = 0.0045**

30. Compute:

800.844 ÷ 0.04 =

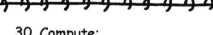

Name _____

45

31-36. Circle the numbers of the problems that are solved correctly.

31. $60.06 \times .10 = 6006$

32. $21.11 \times 4.0 = 8444.0$

33. $.07 \times .008 = 0.00056$

34. $8.10 \div .9 = 9.0$

35. $36.066 \div .006 = 60.11$

36. $30,000 \div .005 = 6,000,000$

37. The product of 41.16 and a number is 16.0524.

What is the number?

Answer: _____

38. Chichi learns that her new skis and boots will cost 2.3 times more than her old equipment.

Her old skis and boots cost $450.

Chichi figures the cost of her new equipment. Does she have it right?

yes   no

39. Solve the equation to find **x.**

$$12\,x = 0.84$$

x = ☐

40. Solve the equation to find **y.**

$$870.055 + y = 930.305$$

y = ☐

Which percentage (from the chart) matches each decimal? Write the %.

_____ 41. 0.897

_____ 42. 0.89907

_____ 43. 0.0897

_____ 44. 89.07

_____ 45. 0.0089077

_____ 46. 0.0879

47. The skier practiced her jumping tricks 4.82 hours a day for 36 days. How long did she practice?

Answer: _____

48. Buster's skis are 110 cm. long.
Leroy's are 60% longer.
How long are Leroy's skis?

Answer: _____

49. 75% of Spike's forty-four ski races are out of his home town. What is the number of races that are in his home town?

Answer: _____

50. When the ski race began, the temperature was 14.5°F.
By the time the race ended, it had risen by 25%.
What was the temperature at the end of the race?
(Round to the nearest tenth of a degree.)

Answer: _____

Name

FRACTIONS, DECIMALS, & PERCENTS

Name _____

Date _____

Possible Correct Answers: 45

Your Correct Answers: _____

Do not use a calculator for any part of this test.

Write each fraction as a decimal.

1. $\frac{6}{7}$ =

2. $\frac{3}{5}$ =

3. $\frac{8}{12}$ =

Write each decimal as a fraction.

4.   0.80 =

5.   0.15 =

6.   4.16 =

7. Leroy has won 38% of the rock climbing contests he has entered this year. Which decimal represents this percentage?

   a. 0.38   c. 0.0038

   b. 38.0   d. 3.8

8. Today Gigi climbed 118% of the distance Spike climbed. Which decimal represents the percentage Gigi has climbed?

   a. 0.118   c. 0.118

   b. 0.00118   d. 1.18

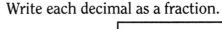
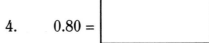

Write each percent as a decimal.

9.   6.03% =

10.   48.5% =

11.   12.7 % =

12.   140.05% =

Write each decimal as a percent.

13.   30.04 =

14.   0.96 =

15.   0.0049 =

16.   37.027 =

6.90   0.069

0.00069

0.0069

6.9   0.69

0.0609

Write the decimal that matches each percent.

_____ 17. 690%

_____ 18. 6.9%

_____ 19. 0.69%

_____ 20. 69%

_____ 21. 0.069%

_____ 22. 6.09%

23. A group of 75 climbers began a long and difficult climbing adventure.
44% of the climbers got some type of injury during the climb.
How many climbers were injured?

Answer: _____

24. Spike and Leroy travel often with their climbing club to scale different
peaks. They've traveled **2895** miles this year. **10%** of their travel has been by bus.
29% has been by train, and **61%** has been by plane. What is the closest estimate
of the number of miles traveled by a method other than plane?

a. 300 miles   b. 1000 miles   c. 1800 miles   d. 1200 miles

25. A number is 3% of 50,000. What is the number? _____

26. 623 is 28% of a number. What is the number? _____

27. 8000 is what % of 200,000? _____

Middle Grade Book of Math Tests

28. Spike is checking the water supply in the bottles. From looking at the bottles, he can tell what fraction of the water is left. He then translates that into a percentage for each bottle. Circle the examples that he has translated into percents accurately (rounded to the nearest whole percent).

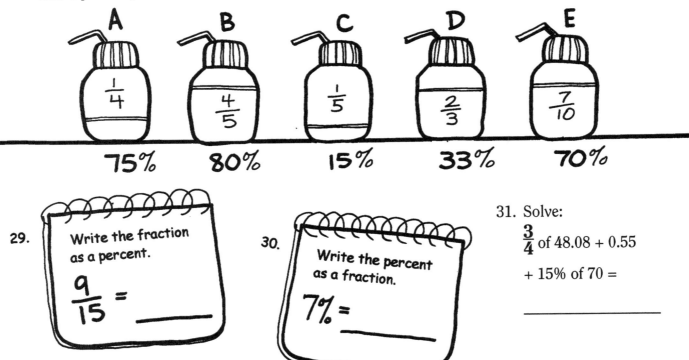

29. Write the fraction as a percent.

$$\frac{9}{15} = \underline{\hspace{2cm}}$$

30. Write the percent as a fraction.

$$7\% = \underline{\hspace{2cm}}$$

31. Solve:

$\frac{3}{4}$ of 48.08 + 0.55

+ 15% of 70 =

_____

Find the missing fraction, percent, or decimal for each blank.

Problem #	Fraction	Decimal	Percent
32.	$\frac{4}{5}$		
33.		0.09	
34.			33.3%
35.	$\frac{8}{20}$		
36.		0.75	
37.		1.6	
38.			2%
39.	$\frac{6}{30}$		

40. On last week's climb, each climber carried a pack that was **28%** of his or her body weight. One climber weighed **78 pounds**. What was the weight of his pack?

    Answer:_____

42. By the end of the first day, the group had climbed **937.5 feet**. This was **15%** of the total distance they would climb to reach the mountain peak. What was the total distance they would climb to reach the top?

    Answer:_____

41. On the first day of the climb, Chichi covered **120%** of the vertical distance of her friend Rosie. Rosie climbed **1350 feet**. How far did Chichi climb?

    Answer:_____

43. By the time they reached the peak, the climbers had drunk **45 quarts** of water. This was **75%** of the water they brought on the trip. How much water was left?

    Answer_____

44. At lunch, Spike ate $\frac{3}{5}$ of his cheese. At dinner, he ate 10% of the remaining cheese. After dinner, how much of his cheese was left? (Give the answer as a fraction, percent, or decimal.)

    Answer: _____

45. Everyone teased Rufus because a large amount of the food weight he carried was made up of candy bars and other junk food. $\frac{6}{8}$ of his 12-pound food bag was indeed junk food.

    a. What percent of the total weight was that?

       Answer: _____

    b. How much did the junk food weigh?

       Answer: _____

Middle Grade Book of Math Tests

MONEY

Name _____

Possible Correct Answers: 25

Date _____

Your Correct Answers: _____

Do not use a calculator for any part of this test.

These six friends are getting ready to go to a basketball game. They each pay a visit to their savings bank to get some money. The chart shows what kinds of bills each one has in his or her bank.

What We've Saved

Name	$100 Bills	$50 Bills	$20 Bills	$10 Bills	$5 Bills	$1 Bills
Chichi	3		9		12	
Roxie		8	2	4		7
Spike	2	2	19	1	2	5
Buster	1	6	3	12	4	6
Rhoda		3	10	35	10	
Rufus			26		11	

1. How much money is in Spike's bank? _____

2. How much money is in Chichi's bank account? _____

3. Who has $119 more than Roxie? _____

4. Whose bank has an amount closest to $500? _____

5. Who has $210 more in twenty and ten-dollar bills than Buster? _____

6. How much money does Rufus have? _____

7. Who has the most money saved? _____

8. How many friends have less money than Chichi? _____

9. Compute:

$ 890.45
— $ 166.80

10. Compute:

$ 4,266.33
+ $ 5,822.49

11. Tickets to the big game cost $11.50 each. Generous Chichi buys a ticket for herself and 12 friends. She pays with two $50 bills and three $20 bills. How much change will she get?

Answer: _____

12. Rufus uses a $20 to buy 3 root beer floats at the game. They cost $1.25 each. How much change will Rufus get?

Answer: _____

13. Choose the correct answer:
(rounded to nearest whole cent)

$583.25 x .03 = _____

a. $ 15.50   c. $ 174.50

b. $ 17.50   d. $ 1.75

14. Choose the correct answer:
(rounded to nearest whole cent)

$6000.00 ÷ 75 = _____

a. $ 80.00   c. $ 8.00

b. $ 800.00   d. $ .80

Name _____

Middle Grade Book of Math Tests

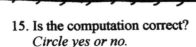

Money

15. Is the computation correct?
Circle yes or no.

$$5 \enclose{longdiv}{\$\,347.30} = \$\ 68.46$$

yes   no

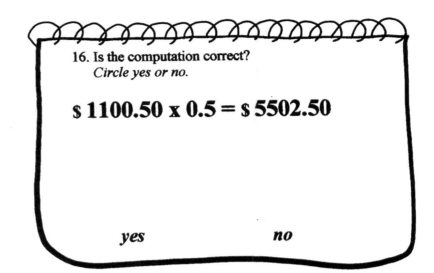

16. Is the computation correct?
Circle yes or no.

$ 1100.50 x 0.5 = $ 5502.50

yes   no

17. The top 5 players on the team make the following salaries each year:
$75,000 $72,000 $78,000 $123,000 $155,000
What is the average salary for these five players?

Answer: _____

18. Four players compared the amount of money they earn in
product endorsements. Their amounts are:
$420,000 $390,000 $650,000 $500,000
What is the average amount earned?

Answer: _____

19. Write and solve an equation to find the amount in the problem below.
Use x to represent the amount of money.

Twenty-five percent interest on an amount of money yields $12,500. What is the amount of money?

_____

Name _____

Middle Grade Book of Math Tests   Copyright ©2001 by Incentive Publications, Inc., Nashville, TN.

20. Solve the equation:

$$x - \$57,999.50 = \$124,001.00$$

$$x = \$ \rule{3cm}{0.4pt}$$

21. Use another operation to verify that this answer is correct.

$$\begin{array}{r} \$\,926.50 \\ \times\ 0.06 \\ \hline \$\,55.59 \end{array}$$

Show your work here:

---

22. The five friends who went to the game spent a total of **$38.45** on food and souvenirs. **1/5** of that amount was spent on food. The rest was spent on souvenirs. How much did they spend on souvenirs?

Answer:

23. Tickets to the game cost **$11.50** each. The total intake of ticket money was **$46,575.00**. How many tickets were sold?

Answer:

24. The average player owns **12** pairs of basketball shoes in a year. Each pair costs between **$100** and **$150**. What is the range of cost for each player in a year for the shoes?

Answer:

---

25. At the end of the game, the booth that sold Grizzly key chains had the following money in the drawer:

14	100-dollar bills
25	50-dollar bills
195	20-dollar bills
310	10-dollar bills
56	1-dollar bills

How much money is this? _____

Name _____

Middle Grade Book of Math Tests

Problem-Solving Skills Checklists

Problem Solving Test #1:

APPROACHES TO PROBLEMS

Test Location: pages 58–61

Skill	*Test Items*
Identify or define a problem	1–5
Identify information unnecessary for problem solution	6, 7
Identify information necessary for problem solution	8, 9
Describe information that is needed for problem solution	10
Identify operations necessary for problem solution	11, 12
Identify operations needed to solve a word problem	13–16
Identify order of operations needed for problem solution	17–20

Problem Solving Test #2:

PROBLEM-SOLVING STRATEGIES

Test Location: pages 62–67

Skill	*Test Items*
Translate a problem into an equation and use it to solve a problem	1–3
Extend a pattern to solve a problem	4–6
Choose and use the correct formula to solve a problem	7–13
Estimate problem solutions	14, 15
Make or label a diagram to solve a problem	16
Use mental math to solve a problem	17, 18
Use logic to solve a problem	19
Solve a problem with trial and error	20, 21
Translate a problem into a proportion for solution	22, 23
Change elements in a problem to a common element for problem solution	24
Choose the best strategy for solving a given problem	25–30

Middle Grade Book of Math Tests

Problem Solving Test #3:

PROBLEMS TO SOLVE, PART 1

Test Location: pages 68–73

Skill	*Test Items*
Write and solve an equation to solve a problem	1–5
Solve multi-step problems	1, 9, 10, 13–15, 21
Solve problems with whole numbers	6–9
Solve problems using trial and error	8
Solve problems with fractions	10, 11, 18
Solve problems involving money	11–16, 27
Solve problems using information from charts and tables	12–20
Estimate problem solutions	17–20
Solve problems with decimals	21, 22
Solve problems with percent	22, 33, 34
Solve problems involving time	23–25
Solve open-ended problems (problems with more than one correct answer)	26–28
Solve problems with rate, ratio, or proportion	29–32
Use a diagram or illustration to assist with problem solution	35

Problem Solving Test #4:

PROBLEMS TO SOLVE, PART 2

Test Location: pages 74–79

Skill	*Test Items*
Use a diagram or illustration to assist with problem solution	1–4, 16
Solve consumer problems involving taxes and discounts	1–4
Use formulas to find perimeter, area, or volume of plane figures	5–10
Solve problems using information from a graph	11–15
Use logic to solve a problem	16
Find combinations or permutations to solve problems	17
Solve probability problems	18–24
Solve multi-step problems	25
Determine the reasonableness of a problem solution	26
Determine the accuracy of problem solutions	27–30

Problem Solving Test #5:

PROBLEM-SOLVING PROCESS

Test Location: pages 80–83

Skill   *Problem-Solving Task*

The problem-solving process test is a test of problem-solving performance. A scoring guide (page 168) is used to enable the adult to give students a score of 1–5 in the areas of Conceptual Understanding, Strategies & Processes, Communication, Correctness (Accuracy of the Answer), and Verification.

Middle Grade Book of Math Tests

APPROACHES TO PROBLEMS

Name _____

Possible Correct Answers: 20

Date _____

Your Correct Answers: _____

Read the examples below (Items 1–5).
If the example is a problem that can be solved,
mark an X in front of it. (Do not solve the problems.)

1. A skydiver spent $633 on her new equipment.
   She sold some old equipment for $485.

2. Four skydivers had 26 years of experience between them.
   How many hours did each one practice?

3. Spike and Chichi wanted to sign up for an 8-week skydiving class.
   The class cost $140 per person or $250 for two persons.
   How much could they save by signing up together?

4. The pilot fueled his plane for $186.00. The tank had 24
   gallons in it, and took 120 gallons more.

5. Three-fourths of all Spike's skydiving friends have never had a skydiving accident.
   Spike has 24 friends who skydive. How many friends have had an accident?

6. Draw a line through information that is NOT needed in order to solve the problem. *(Do not solve the problem.)*

Each of the 136 skydivers who jumped today has
3 parachutes. 80% of these parachutes are new.
38% of them were bought at the Sky Thrills Shop.
50% of the chutes have red and white stripes on the
canopy. How many of the parachutes are not new?

Middle Grade Book of Math Tests

Copyright ©2001 by Incentive Publications, Inc., Nashville, TN.

7. Circle the letters of the information that is NOT needed to answer this question.

How many balloons were too damaged for repair?

a. During the year, 386 damaged balloons were brought into the repair shop.
b. Repairs on most of the balloons cost over $200.
c. 35% of the balloons were damaged beyond repair.
d. 18% of the damaged balloon had problems with their heaters.

8. What information is needed to answer the question below? (Circle the letters.)

How many spectators watched some or all of the Steeplechase Balloon Race?

a. 4,250 watched in the morning.
b. Many balloon-watchers went home around noon.
c. 68 balloons dropped out of the race.
d. The afternoon crowd was twice the size of the morning crowd.

9. What information is needed to answer this question? (Circle the letters.)

What fraction of the balloons finished the race?

a. $\frac{1}{2}$ of the balloons had troubles during the race.

b. **256** balloons entered the race.

c. $\frac{1}{4}$ of the balloons did not finish the race.

d. Three balloons tied for second place.

e. The wind was good for ballooning today.

10. Some information is missing from the problem below. What information is needed in order to find a solution? Write your answer.

Spectators at the balloon race drove a total of 62,594 miles following the balloons around the city. On the average, how far did each car drive?

Missing: _____

Name _____

Middle Grade Book of Math Tests

11–12. Write the signs to show what operations need to be done in order to find the solution that is shown:

11. $100{,}000 \;\square\; 100 \;\square\; 11 = 10{,}000{,}011$

12. $555{,}555 \;\square\; 11 \;\square\; 50{,}505 = 0$

Determine what operations are needed to solve the problems below. Do NOT solve the problems.

13. What operation is needed to solve this problem? _____
Last summer, Spike found time to go sky surfing 35 times.
This summer, the number of times he went sky surfing was 60% of last summer's number.
How many times did he sky surf this summer?

14. What operation is needed to solve this problem? _____
On the average, each member of Leroy's sky-surfing team spent $130
on visits to doctors and emergency rooms. There are 26 members
on the team. How much did they spend all together?

15. What operation is needed to solve this problem? _____
Each year, more adventurers try the extreme sport of sky surfing.
In Spike's area, 840 more tried it this year than last year.
This year, 1035 tried the sport for the first time.
How many tried the sport for the first time last year ?

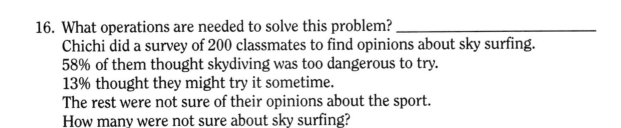

16. What operations are needed to solve this problem? _____
Chichi did a survey of 200 classmates to find opinions about sky surfing.
58% of them thought skydiving was too dangerous to try.
13% thought they might try it sometime.
The rest were not sure of their opinions about the sport.
How many were not sure about sky surfing?

Name _____

60

17. What is the correct order for performing operations to solve this problem?

Spike decided to try walking across a 276-foot high-wire.

He walked $\frac{1}{3}$ of the distance, and froze.

Gradually, he inched backwards to the beginning.

How much distance did Spike cover?

   a. multiply, then add

   b. add, then multiply

   c. multiply, then subtract

   d. subtract, then multiply

18. What is the correct order for performing operations to solve this problem?

Last year, 120 adventuresome folks signed up to learn high-wire walking.
60% of those who took the class dropped out.
50% of those who stayed did a high-wire walk only one time.
How many walked the wire more than once?

   a. multiply, then add

   b. add, then multiply, then add

   c. multiply, subtract, then multiply again

   d. divide, then multiply

19. What is the correct order for performing operations to solve this problem?

High-wire walking is an expensive sport.
Spike paid $500 for lessons, $35 a day to rent equipment,
and $40 a day for insurance.
He has only $800 saved.
Can he do this sport for 3 days?

   a. multiply, then add, then add   c. multiply, then divide

   b. add, then multiply   d. subtract, then multiply

20. What operation should be done first in order to solve this problem?

Spike stayed on the high wire for 13.9 minutes.

Sam's walk took $2\frac{1}{2}$ times as long as Spike's.

Roxie's walk was 3.7 minutes longer than Sam's.

How long did Roxie's walk take?

   a. add

   b. subtract

   c. multiply

   d. divide

Name

Middle Grade Book of Math Tests

PROBLEM-SOLVING STRATEGIES

Name _____

Possible Correct Answers: 30

Date _____

Your Correct Answers: _____

Translate each problem into an equation. Write and solve the equation.

1. The fishing was good today. 132 fish were caught.
   The friends who were fishing used different boats.
   Each boat brought in 44 fish. How many boats were there?

   Equation: _____

   Solution: _____

2. One hundred forty-eight swimmers started a race.
   Nineteen stopped the race because of cramps.
   Twelve dropped out because of sunburn.
   Seventeen did not finish due to fatigue. How many finished the race?

   Equation: _____   Solution: _____

3. A group rented 6 boats. They also bought $18 worth of gasoline. They paid a total of $258. What was the rental cost for each boat?

   Equation: _____   Solution: _____

4. Fill in the numbers to continue the pattern.

   250   245   235   [ ]   200   175   [ ]   [ ]

5. Fill in the numbers to continue the pattern.

   1000   900   700   400   [ ]   −500   [ ]

62

6. Find the pattern to solve the problem.

When Leroy began rowing practice, he could row 3 miles per hour.
After one week of practice, he could row at a rate 30% faster.
In Week #2, his rate was 20% better than at the end of Week #1.
In Week #3, his rate was 10% better than at the end of Week #2.
What was his rate at the end of Week #4?

Answer :_____

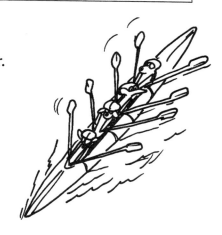

Use a formula to find the perimeter, area, or volume of the described in problems 7–13.

7. Find the perimeter.

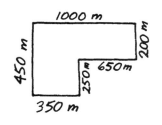

1000 m
450 m
200 m
650 m
250 m
350 m

P = _____

8. Find the area.

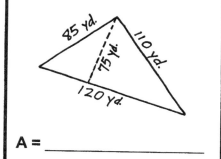

85 yd.
110 yd.
75 yd.
120 yd.

A = _____

9. Find the area.

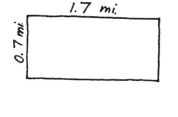

1.7 mi.
0.7 mi.

A = _____

10. Find the volume.

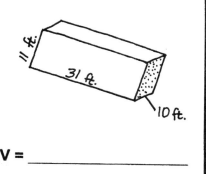

11 ft.
31 ft.
10 ft.

V = _____

11. Find the volume.

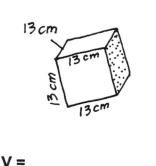

13 cm
13 cm
13 cm
13 cm

V = _____

12. Find the volume.

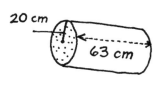

20 cm
63 cm

V = _____

13. A pond is 70 feet long, 35 feet wide , and 20 feet deep.

a. What is its perimeter?   P =_____

b. What is its surface area?   A =_____

c. What volume of water does it hold?   V = _____

Name _____

Middle Grade Book of Math Tests

14. Estimate the answer.

Leroy spends a lot of time just floating on the lake. He does this about 3.8 hours a day, six days a week. Over a 12-week summer, about how much time does Leroy spend floating?

Estimate: _____

15. Estimate the answer.

Chichi's new water skis had a price of $113. Her life vest was priced at $34. She got a 20% discount on both of them. About how much did she pay?

Estimate: _____

16. Label the diagram to solve the problem.
The five divers are Trixie, Minnie, Char, Gigi, and Sal. Sal is on the right end. Gigi is between Char and Trixie. Char is not next to Sal. Trixie is not next to Minnie. Char is next to Minnie. Which diver is Minnie?

Circle: **A**   **B**   **C**   **D**   **E**

A   B   C   D   E

17. Use mental math to solve this problem.
Leroy caught a fish weighing 118 pounds. Spike's biggest fish weighed 30 pounds more than $\frac{1}{2}$ the weight of Leroy's fish. What is the weight of Spike's fish?

Answer: _____

18. Use mental math to solve this problem.

The rowing team entered a race at a lake far from home. They traveled 14 hours and 35 minutes, arriving at 4:15 p.m. on Friday. When did they leave home?

Answer: _____

19. Use logic to solve this problem.

At this point in the race, four boats are far out in front of the rest. The Speed Kings boat is in the lead. The Kentucky Splash Team is not next to the Atlanta Racers. The Water Wizards are not in second place. Could the Water Wizards be in fourth place?

Answer: _____

Name _____

Middle Grade Book of Math Tests

20. Use trial and error to solve the problem below.

    Spike's diving coach is 5 times Spike's age. In 8 years, the coach will be 3 times Spike's age at that time.

    What are their ages now?

    Spike:_____

    Coach: _____

21. Use trial and error to solve the problem below.

    An even 3-digit multiple of 9 is > 400 and < 500. All the digits are different.
    The digit in the tens place is an odd number. No digits are > 4.

    What is the number?

    Answer: _____

22. To solve the problem, translate the facts into a proportion.

    3 out of 16 swimmers in the race suffer regularly from ear infections.
    At this rate, how many swimmers in the 240 who started the race suffer from ear infections?

    Proportion: _____

    Answer: _____

23. To solve the problem, translate the facts into a proportion.

    5 out of every 12 divers at the diving meet had missed at least 2 weeks of training because of an injury during the past year. If 70 divers at the meet missed this much training due to injuries, how many divers, total, were taking part in the meet?

    Proportion: _____

    Answer: _____

Name _____

Middle Grade Book of Math Tests

24. To solve the problem, change facts to a common element. (Show your work.)

From the time she left home, it took Chichi 3 hours and 15 minutes to get to the lake.

It took her $\frac{3}{4}$ of an hour to unload her canoe and other equipment.

It took her 15 minutes to get canoe into the water.

It took her 90 seconds to get her suit on.

It took another 120 seconds for her to get into the boat and start paddling.

From the time she left home,
   how long was it before she started paddling?

Answer: _____

One day, Chichi paddled her canoe 12 miles. For the next several days, she paddled an average of 14 miles a day. After several days, she had covered a total of 252 miles. How many days did she paddle?

25. Choose the best strategy to solve the problem above. (Circle one letter.)

   a. Make a graph.
   b. Use trial and error.
   c. Translate facts into a proportion.
   d. Estimate the answer.

   e. Draw a diagram.
   f. Use a formula.
   g. Translate the problem into an equation.
   h. Find and extend a pattern.

Four divers are lined up in order of their height. Fritz is shorter than C.J., who is taller than Bud. Moe is shorter than Fritz. Moe is not standing next to C.J. Who is the shortest?

26. Choose the best strategy to solve the problem above. (Circle one letter.)

   a. Make a graph.
   b. Use trial and error.
   c. Translate facts into a proportion.
   d. Estimate the answer.

   e. Draw a diagram.
   f. Use a formula.
   g. Translate the problem into an equation.
   h. Find and extend a pattern.

Name _____

66

During every 4 hours of work time, a lifeguard rescues 6 swimmers in trouble. At this rate, how many swimmers would be rescued in a 6-day work week of 8 hours a day?

27. Choose the best strategy to solve the problem above.
   a. Use mental math.
   b. Use trial and error.
   c. Translate facts into a proportion.
   d. Translate the problem into an equation.
   e. Draw a diagram.
   f. Use a formula.
   g. Estimate the answer.
   h. Find and extend a pattern.

A ferryboat crossing the lake has 38 rows of seats. Each group has 19 seats. About how many people could the boat carry in 11 trips?

28. Choose the best strategy to solve the problem above.
   a. Use mental math
   b. Use trial and error.
   c. Translate facts into a proportion.
   d. Estimate the answer.
   e. Draw a diagram.
   f. Use a formula.
   g. Translate the problem into an equation.
   h. Find and extend a pattern.

For exercise, Spike paddles his canoe around the outside edge of the lake every morning. The lake is shaped like a right triangle with sides of 800 feet, 960 feet, and 1300 feet. How far does Spike paddle?

29. Choose the best strategy to solve the problem above.
   a. Make a graph.
   b. Use trial and error.
   c. Translate facts into an equation .
   d. Estimate the answer.
   e. Draw a diagram.
   f. Use a formula.
   g. Guess & check.
   h. Find and extend a pattern.

Leroy is trying to catch 20 fish before dark. It will be dark at 8:15 p.m., which is 9 hours and 30 minutes from now. What time is it now?

30. Choose the best strategy to solve the problem above.
   a. Use mental math.
   b. Use trial and error.
   c. Translate facts into a proportion.
   d. Estimate the answer.
   e. Draw a diagram.
   f. Use a formula.
   g. Guess & check.
   h. Find and extend a pattern.

Name _____

Middle Grade Book of Math Tests

PROBLEMS TO SOLVE, PART 1

Name _____   Possible Correct Answers: 35

Date _____   Your Correct Answers: _____

Write and solve an equation to find the answer for each problem (1–5).
Use x to represent the unknown quantity.

1. Spike held auditions for his new band. The first day, he listened to 13 singers and guitar players. The second day, he listened to 28 singers and drummers. He turned down most of those who auditioned. He invited the remaining seven to join the band. How many did he turn away?

   _____

   _____

2. A number, when added to $6\frac{1}{2}$, yields $12\frac{5}{8}$. What is the number?

   _____

   _____

   _____

4. The difference between 400 and a certain number is 87.5. What is the number?

   _____

   _____

3. The sum of 0.33 and another number is 3.3 greater than 3.66. What is the other number?

   _____

   _____

   _____

5. The product of 12 and 250 is 2700 greater than a number. What is the number?

   _____

   _____

   _____

68

Find the answer for each problem below.

6. The band is 18 concerts short of finishing this year's tour of 53 concerts. They perform 22 songs in each concert. How many songs have they performed so far in their tour?

    Answer:_____

7. The largest concert hall on the tour is the Houndsville Dome. The dome can hold 14,800 fans in 80 sections of seats. How many seats are there in each section?

    Answer: _____

8. Find the number of fans who attended the concert at the Woofer Auditorium. It is a 4-digit even number. The number is < 5000. All digits are different, and all are even numbers. The sum of the digits is 18. The largest digit is in the ones place and the smallest is in the tens place.

    Answer: _____

9. Here are the miles that the band traveled to arrive at last week's concerts: Sunday–350; Monday–195; Tuesday–400; Wednesday–70; Thursday–310; Friday–280; Saturday–355. What is the average number of miles traveled in a day?

    Answer: _____

10. Before Monday's concert, the band ate $7\frac{1}{2}$ pizzas. After the concert they ate $\frac{2}{3}$ of that amount. How much pizza did they eat all together?

    Answer: _____

11. The band spent $8400 on new speakers this year. Last year they spent $\frac{5}{8}$ of this amount. How much did they spend last year?

    Answer: _____

Name _____

Middle Grade Book of Math Tests

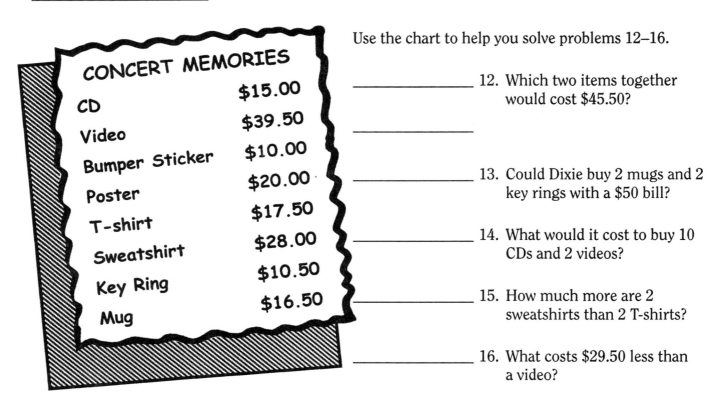

CONCERT MEMORIES

CD	$15.00
Video	$39.50
Bumper Sticker	$10.00
Poster	$20.00
T-shirt	$17.50
Sweatshirt	$28.00
Key Ring	$10.50
Mug	$16.50

Use the chart to help you solve problems 12–16.

_____ 12. Which two items together would cost $45.50?

_____

_____ 13. Could Dixie buy 2 mugs and 2 key rings with a $50 bill?

_____ 14. What would it cost to buy 10 CDs and 2 videos?

_____ 15. How much more are 2 sweatshirts than 2 T-shirts?

_____ 16. What costs $29.50 less than a video?

Using the table below, estimate the answers for questions 17–20.

Ticket Sales at Concerts

Concert Location	1997	1998	1999	2000
Houndsville Dome	7685	9205	10,150	6050
Canine City Center	2316	4120	2087	3210
Dogs' Corners Arena	8115	3950	2977	6710
Wooferville Arena	4608	3050	6150	5900
Muttsville Stadium	4955	5116	6210	3710

_____ 17. Which city had the best ticket sales over the 4-year period?

_____ 18. In 1999, which city sold about $\frac{1}{3}$ as many tickets as Muttsville?

_____ 19. Which city sold about 1300 more tickets in 2000 than in 1997?

_____ 20. Which city sold about 22,000 tickets over the 4-year period?

21. **7 band members** drank **3.6 liters** of water during each concert for **19 concerts**. What is the total amount of water consumed by these band members?

Answer:_____

22. The longest song on the band's latest CD is **5.007 minutes** long. The shortest song is **67%** as long. How long is the shortest song?

Answer:_____

23. After the concert, the band left Toledo **at 1:40 a.m.** They traveled **14 hours and 25 minutes** to Oklahoma City. What time did they arrive?

24. When Friday's concert ended, the band figured they had **19 hours and 45 minutes** until the next concert began. Saturday's concert began at **7:30 p.m.** What time did Friday's concert end?

Answer:_____

25. After the last Saturday night concert of the season, Spike went straight to bed. He was asleep within **10 minutes**, and he slept **28 hours and 38 minutes**. Saturday's concert ended at **11:55 p.m.** When did Spike awake?

Answer: Day_____

Time_____

26. Spike's drummer, Bongo, has been playing drums for a number of years. Here are some facts about that number:
    - It is a 2-digit number under 40. Both digits are odd.
    - The sum of the digits is 10.
    - Their product is an odd number.
    Find two different numbers that this could be.

    _____   _____

27. Chichi went to buy some popcorn at the concert's intermission. She reached in her pocket and pulled out 21 coins. The coins totaled $1.85.
    Describe two different combinations of coins she could have had in her hand.

    COINS

    _____

    _____

28. Wally and Gus are two fans who came to the concert together. The sum of their ages is between 20 and 40. The product of their ages is 108.
    How old are they? Find two different possible solutions.

    _____   _____

29. A songwriter wrote **5** hit songs in her first **6** years of songwriting. At this rate, how many hits would she write in **30** years?

    Answer:_____

30. The band members got **72** requests for interviews in a year. At this rate, how many requests did they get in a **3-month** period?

    Answer:_____

31. Twenty fans fainted during the first **8** concerts of the band's tour. At this rate, how many would faint during the next **48** concerts?

    Answer:_____

Name _____

72

32. It was a long way from Denver to the next concert. The band's bus traveled 14.5 hours at an average rate of 72 miles per hour. How far did they travel?

    Answer: _____

33. Spike's last guitar was a bargain. He got 25% off the price. Spike paid $171.00. What was the original price?

    Answer: _____

34. Spike's band surprises their listeners by throwing in a few songs that are not rock & roll. At the last concert, 25% of their 20 songs were country & western. How many country & western songs did they play?

    Answer: _____

35. At the end of the concert, five singers on stage each shake the hand of every other singer. If you want to find out how many handshakes this will involve, which one of the figures would be the most helpful?

    A.   B.   C.   D.   E. none of these

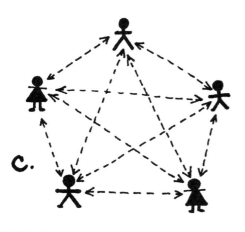

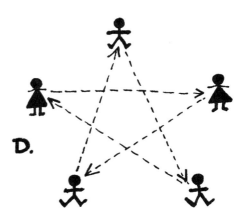

Middle Grade Book of Math Tests

PROBLEMS TO SOLVE, PART 2

Name _____

Date _____

Possible Correct Answers: 30

Your Correct Answers: _____

Use the illustrations and the prices to solve problems 1–6.

BACK PACK
$189.50

CAMP STOVE
$59.50

TENT
$99.00

BOOTS
$89.00

SLEEPING BAG
$218.00

WATER BOTTLES
2/for $18.00

1. Spike can get a 45% discount on the backpack and a 25% discount on the tent. Which item will cost him less?

Answer: _____

2. What is the cost of the sleeping bag with a 15% discount plus 5% sales tax?

Answer: _____

3. Leroy wants to purchase boots and a stove. What will he pay (with a 5% tax)?

Answer: _____

4. What will Leroy pay for a sleeping bag and 8 water bottles with a 15% discount and 5% tax?

Answer: _____

5. This fire circle has a diameter of **2.3 meters**.

What is the circumference?

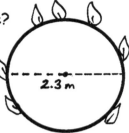

2.3 m

C = _____

6. What is the area of the circle?

A = _____

7. A triangular tarp to go beneath a tent has sides of these lengths:
72 in., 95 in., and **80 in.**

What is the perimeter?

P = _____

115 m

50 m

50 m

20 m

35 m

50 m

50 m

60 m

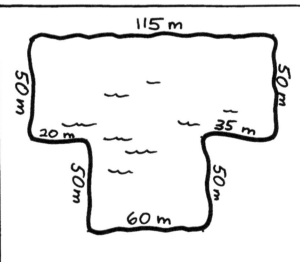

8. A camper hikes around the outer edge of this pond **five** times.
How far does she walk?

Answer_____

9. What is the surface area of the pond above?

A = _____

10. The pond is **18 feet** deep.
What is the volume of the water it holds?

V = _____

Use the graph to solve problems 11–15.

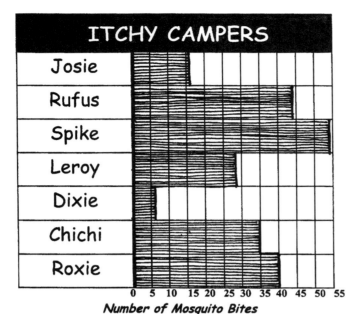

ITCHY CAMPERS

Josie
Rufus
Spike
Leroy
Dixie
Chichi
Roxie

0 5 10 15 20 25 30 35 40 45 50 55
Number of Mosquito Bites

11. Who has about $\frac{1}{2}$ the number of Chichi's bites?

_____

12. Whose number of bites is $\frac{1}{9}$ of Spike's?

_____

13. Whose number is $\frac{7}{8}$ of Roxie's?

_____

14. About how many bites does the group have all together? _____

15. Who has 16 fewer than Rufus? _____

16. Use the illustration below to help solve the logic problem.

Each of the four hikers has one of these ailments: blisters, bruises on the shoulder, a swollen ankle, and bee stings. Read the clues, then circle the answer to the question:

Which hiker has the swollen ankle?   **A   B   C   D**

The hiker with the bee stings is wearing a hat.
The hiker with the blisters has no hat.
The hiker with bruised shoulders has no sunglasses.
The hiker with a swollen ankle not wearing long pants.
The hiker with the bruised shoulders has no hat.

Name _____

76

17. When Leroy goes to rent some camping equipment, he has some choices of colors for backpacks and sleeping bags. The backpacks come in gray, orange, or brown. The sleeping bags are green, blue, or red. He rents one pack and one sleeping bag. How many different combinations of colors are possible?

a. 3   b. 6   c. 5   d. 9

Spike has carried a good-sized load of snacks in his pack. Right now, he has 20 chocolate bars, 16 bars of taffy, and 12 granola bars. If he reaches into his bag without looking and grabs one bar, what is the probability . . .

18. . . . that it will be chocolate? _____

19. . . . that it will be granola? _____

20. . . . that it will be taffy? _____

21. . . . that it will NOT be chocolate? _____

22. There are six hikers: Spike, Roxie, Rufus, Leroy, Dixie, and Chichi. They walk along the path in pairs. Name all the possible pairs:

_____

_____

23. Every time the hikers make camp for the night they flip a coin to see who has to build the fire. If they flip the coin 10 times on their trip, how many times is it likely to come up "tails"?

a. 10   b. 5   c. 20   d. 3

Name _____

Middle Grade Book of Math Tests

24. When the campers set up their tents, they like to put tarps over the tents to protect them from the rain. A group of campers has brought **8** tarps. **3** of them leak. Rufus grabs a tarp out of the pile. What is the probability that it will be a leaky tarp?

a. $\frac{1}{3}$ b. $\frac{8}{3}$

c. $\frac{3}{8}$ d. $\frac{11}{3}$

e. $\frac{3}{5}$ f. $\frac{3}{11}$

g. none of these

25. One night Leroy and his friends stopped at a big campground. **85** campers were getting ready to spend the night there. When rain started pouring down, everyone crowded into the tents. **Six** campers could fit into each tent. How many tents were needed to protect all the campers?

Answer:_____

26. Each of six campers brought an assortment of food. They each brought about 12 packages of dried dinners; 6 packages of dried fruit; 23 sticks of jerky, 30 pieces of candy, and 9 packages of cereal.

Which of these is a reasonable estimate of the number of food items brought by the whole group?

  a. 80

  b. 8000

  c. 1500

  d. 500

  e. 800

  f. none of these

**Check the accuracy of each problem solution.
If the answer is incorrect, write the correct answer.**

27. The hikers covered **36,555 feet**
in their walk today.
2/5 of the distance was uphill.
How many feet of the hike were uphill?

Solution: **9,111 feet were uphill.**

28. The lake has a surface area of 35,000 square feet.
35% of the lake is in the sun.
What part of the lake is NOT in the sun?

Solution: **22,750 square feet are not in the sun.**

29. Seven friends hiked these distances over 7 days:

Day # 1:	4.8 miles	Day # 5:	15.0 miles
Day # 2:	10.2 miles	Day # 6:	12.3 miles
Day # 3:	9.5 miles	Day # 7:	9.9 miles
Day # 4:	6.9 miles		

What is the average distance they hiked each day?

Solution: **The average distance is 9.8 miles.**

30. At the end of the trip, Spike was exhausted. He slept
from noon on Saturday until **12:15** a.m. on Tuesday.
How long did he sleep?

Solution: **Spike slept 24 hours and 15 minutes.**

Name _____

Middle Grade Book of Math Tests

PROBLEM-SOLVING PROCESS

Name _____　　Possible Correct Answers: 25

Date _____　　Your Correct Answers: _____

The purpose of this test is to find out how well you can solve a math problem and explain the way you solved it.

DIRECTIONS:

1) Choose ONE of the problems on the next page (page 2).
2) Use the space on pages 3 and 4 to solve the problem.
3) Show your answer and ALL your work clearly.
4) Make sure that a reader can tell HOW you solved the problem. Use diagrams, pictures, symbols, or words to show the steps you went through to solve the problem.
5) When you finish, review your work and find a way to show that the answer is correct. You might work the problem a second way to show this.

- Your problem solving will be scored in the following five areas.
- You can receive 1-5 points on each trait.
- A good problem-solving example will receive at least 3 points in each trait.

UNDERSTANDING THE CONCEPT: Show that you understand what the problem is and that you can change the word problem into mathematical symbols, numbers, or ideas. Show that you can find and use the information from the problem that is needed to solve it.

STRATEGIES & PROCESSES: Show all the numbers, diagrams, symbols, equations, or pictures that you used to solve the problem. Label all diagrams and pictures. Show these in the order you used them. The strategies you choose need to be well-fitted to the problem.

COMMUNICATION: Clearly show the process (steps) and strategies you used with numbers, symbols, diagrams, pictures, and/or words.

CORRECTNESS: Give a final answer that is a clear answer to the question asked in the problem. Your final answer needs to be correct.

VERIFICATION: After the problem is solved, find another way to solve or check the problem to verify or defend your answer.

Middle Grade Book of Math Tests

PROBLEMS TO SOLVE (Choose one.)

PROBLEM # 1

Eight members of a rock band have a mean (average) height of 56 inches. The heights of seven of the members are: 62 inches; 56 inches; 5 feet and 1 inch; 49 inches; 60 inches, 5 feet and 8 inches; and 58 inches. What is the height of the eighth band member?

PROBLEM # 2

After basketball practice on Friday, five players headed for the showers. Only one shower was working, so Slim, Sam, Jim, Sly, and Shorty took turns. Jim showered ahead of Slim. Shorty showered ahead of Sam but behind Slim. Slim showered ahead of three others. Sam showered ahead of Sly. Who showered last?

PROBLEM # 3

Spike spent $350 on new skis and boots. Then he bought a new jacket for $89.50 and goggles for $39.00. He paid an 8% sales tax on all his purchases. When he sold his old equipment, he made enough money to pay for all but $110.00 of the new purchases. How much did he get from the old equipment?

PROBLEM # 4

A ping pong ball factory packages ping pong balls in individual boxes that are 3 x 3 x 3 inches. How many of these will fit into a large shipping container that is 17 inches tall x 18 inches wide x 20 inches long?

PROBLEM # 5

Two runners, Skip and Sam, have the same two digits in their ages, but the digits are reversed. The sum of their ages is a number that is $1/14$ of the product of their ages less 34. What are their ages?

PROBLEM # 6

A team of snowboarders traveled to a competition far from home. They left their hometown in the Eastern Time Zone. They traveled 59 hours and 18 minutes to a ski area that was in the Mountain Time Zone. They arrived at 12:40 p.m. Mountain Time on Thursday. When did they leave home? (Give the day and time.)

PROBLEM # 7

The new dance floor is ready for painting and varnishing. First, the painters paint a 6-inch wide stripe around the outside edge of the floor. Next, they spread two coats of varnish on the entire surface area of the floor (not on top of the painted stripe). Each gallon can of paint or varnish covers 500 square feet of surface. How many more cans of varnish will they need than cans of paint?

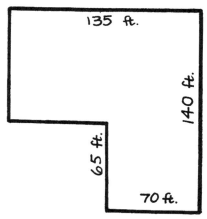

Name _____

Problem # _____

_____

_____

_____

_____

_____

_____

_____

_____

_____

_____

_____

_____

_____

_____

_____

_____

_____

_____

_____

_____

_____

If you need more space, continue your work on the next page.

Name _____

Problem # _____

_____

_____

_____

_____

_____

_____

_____

_____

_____

_____

_____

_____

_____

_____

_____

_____

_____

_____

_____

_____

_____

_____

_____

_____

_____

_____

_____

_____

Geometry & Measurement Skills Checklists

Geometry & Measurement Test #1:
PLANE GEOMETRY
Test Location: pages 86–93

Skill	*Test Items*
Identify and describe points, lines, line segments, rays, and planes	1–9
Identify and distinguish between parallel, perpendicular, and intersecting lines	7, 8, 10–12
Estimate or compare measure of angles	9, 19–21
Identify different kinds of angles	13–18
Identify properties of a circle	22–26
Identify and define kinds of triangles	27–30
Identify congruent and similar figures	31–35
Identify and define different polygons	36–41
Recognize properties of different plane figures	42–51
Distinguish among different quadrilaterals	45–51
Identify symmetrical figures	52
Identify congruent angles	53–56
Choose correct formulas for finding area and perimeter of plane figures	57, 58
Find the perimeter or circumference of plane figures	59, 61, 63, 65, 67, 69
Find the area of plane figures	60, 62, 64, 66, 68, 70
Compare areas of plane figures	71
Identify figure slides, flips, and turns	72
Recognize and draw transformations of plane figures	73–75

Geometry & Measurement Test #2:
SPACE GEOMETRY
Test Location: pages 94–99

Geometry & Measurement Test #3:
MEASUREMENT
Test Location: 100–109

PLANE GEOMETRY

Name _____

Possible Correct Answers: 75

Date _____

Your Correct Answers: _____

Circle one or more answers for each.

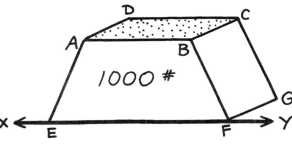

Use the diagram for questions 1 - 9.

Weight Room

1. XY is
  a. a line segment
  b. a line
  c. a ray
  d. a plane
	4. B is
	  a. a line
	  b. a point
	  c. a ray
	  d. a line segment
		7. AB is parallel to
		  a. BC
		  b. CD
		  c. FG
		  d. CG

2. These are line segments:
  a. FY
  b. AB
  c. BF
  d. EA
  e. AC
	5. ADC is
	  a. a plane
	  b. an angle
	  c. a line
	  d. a line segment
	  e. a ray
		8. EF is not parallel to
		  a. DC
		  b. AB
		  c. FG
		  d. BC
		  e. AD

3. EX is
  a. a line segment
  b. a line
  c. an angle
  d. a ray
	6. ABFE is
	  a. a plane
	  b. an angle
	  c. a line segment
	  d. a ray
		9. AEF is
		  a. larger than ADC
		  b. smaller than ABC
		  c. equal to EFB
		  d. equal to BAE

Use the line segments below for questions 10–12.
Circle the correct letter for each answer.

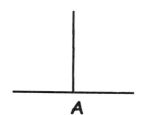

A

B

C   **D**

10. Which pair of line segments is **parallel**?

A   B   C   D

11. Which pair is **perpendicular**?

A   B   C   D

12. Which pair of line segments **intersect**?

A   B   C   D

Use these angles for questions 13–18.

Write one or more letters for each answer.

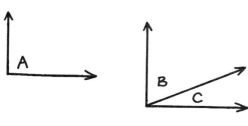

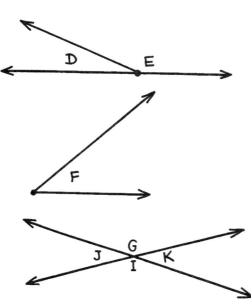

13. Which angles are right angles?

_____

14. Which angles are obtuse angles?

_____

15. Which angles are acute angles?

_____

16. Name one pair of supplementary angles.

_____

17. Which angles are complementary angles?

_____

18. Name one pair of corresponding angles.

_____

Middle Grade Book of Math Tests

19. This angle is about
    a. 20°
    b. 95°
    c. 150°
    d. 45°

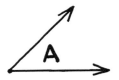

20. This angle is about
    a. 60°
    b. 175°
    c. 10°
    d. 90°

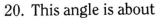

21. Which angle is about 100°? _____

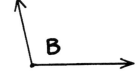

Use this diagram for questions 22–26.

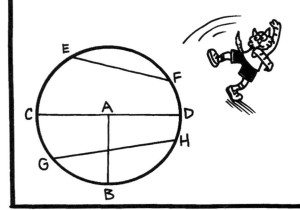

22. Name the diameter. _____

23. Name a chord. _____

24. Name two radii. _____

_____

25. Name a central angle. _____

26. Is EA an arc? _____

Use these triangles for questions 27–30.
Write the numbers from the triangles for the answers.

27. Which ones are scalene? _____

28. Which are isosceles? _____

29. Which are right? _____

30. Which are equilateral? _____

Name _____

Middle Grade Book of Math Tests

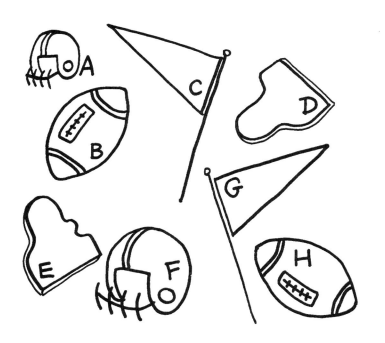

Use the pictures below for questions 31–35.
Answer T (for true) or F (for false).

_____ 31. F is congruent to A.

_____ 32. D is congruent to E.

_____ 33. A is similar to F.

_____ 34. B is similar to F.

_____ 35. G is congruent to C.

Use the signs below for questions 36–41.
Write the letters of the correct answers.

36. Which figures are rhombuses? _____

37. Which figure is a hexagon? _____

38. Which figures are parallelograms? _____

39. Which figure is a pentagon? _____

40. Which figure is a trapezoid? _____

41. Which figures are rectangles? _____

Name _____

Middle Grade Book of Math Tests

Choose the correct answer for questions 42–44.

42. Spike's bowling team pennant is a triangle with only two equal sides. This triangle is
   a. equilateral
   b. isosceles
   c. scalene

44. The bowling alley has a new floor, patterned with figures. Each is a rhombus with four equal angles.
   These figures are
      a. trapezoids
      b. squares
      c. hexagons
      d. pentagons
      e. octagons

43. The design on the team's new bowling shirts is a polygon with seven sides. This figure is
      a. a hexagon
      b. an octagon
      c. a nonagon
      d. a decagon
      e. a heptagon

Write T (true) or F (false) for statements 45–51.

_____45. All rectangles have 4 right angles.

_____46. A square is a rectangle.

_____47. All parallelograms have 4 equal angles.

_____48. All rectangles have 4 equal angles.

_____49. A rectangle is a quadrilateral.

_____50. A rhombus is always a square.

_____51. All quadrilaterals are rectangles.

Name _____

Middle Grade Book of Math Tests

52. Which figures below are symmetrical? (Circle the letters.)

A   B   C   D   E   F   G   H

Use this figure for questions 53–56.

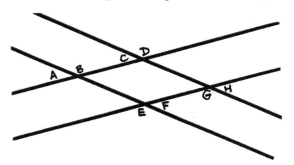

53. Is angle B congruent to angle D? _____

54. Is angle C congruent to angle H? _____

55. Is angle E congruent to angle F? _____

56. Is angle F congruent to angle H? _____

57. What formula should the players use to find the distance around the outside of the volleyball court?

    a. $2(l + w)$ c. $l \times w$

    b. $(l + w)^2$ d. $2 \times l \times w$

58. What formula should the players use to find the surface area of the court?

    a. $\frac{1}{2}l \times w$ c. $l \times w \times h$

    b. $l \times w^2$ d. $l \times w$

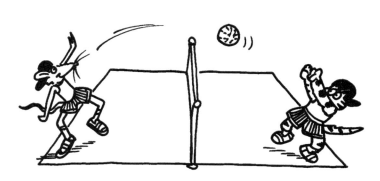

Name _____

Middle Grade Book of Math Tests

Find the **perimeter** (or circumference) and **area** for each figure.

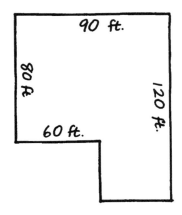

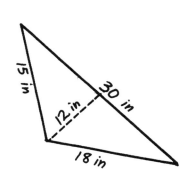

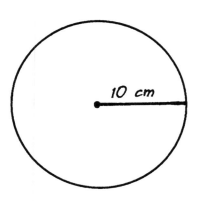

59. P = _____

60. A = _____

61. P = _____

62. A = _____

63. C = _____

64. A = _____

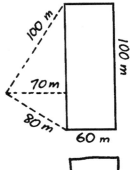

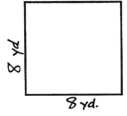

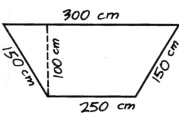

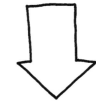

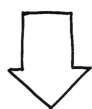

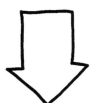

65. P = _____

66. A = _____

67. P = _____

68. A = _____

69. P = _____

70. A = _____

Middle Grade Book of Math Tests

71. Which has the greatest area?

a. a boxing "ring" that is 21-ft square

b. a tennis court that is 131 ft x 65.5 ft.

c. a volleyball court that is 18m x 9m

d. a badminton court that is 6.1 m x 13.4 m

72. Label each diagram **slide, flip,** or **turn** to describe the transformation shown.

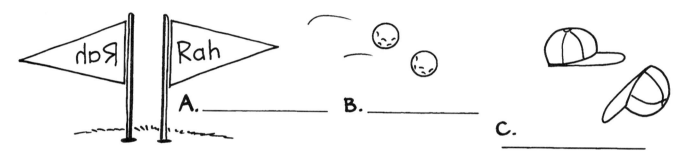

A. _____ B. _____

C. _____

73. Draw a **turn** of this figure.

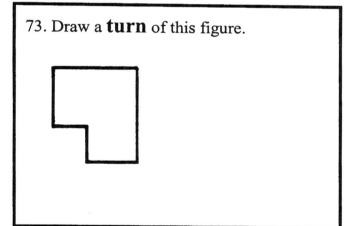

74. Draw a **flip** of this figure.

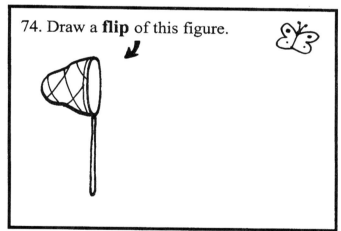

75. Draw a **slide** of this figure.

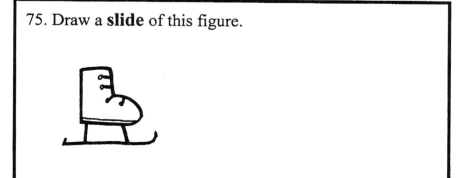

Name _____

93

SPACE GEOMETRY

Name _____

Date _____

Possible Correct Answers: 40

Your Correct Answers: _____

Which figure is which?

Write the name of each space figure.

1. _____

2. _____

3. _____

4. _____

5. _____

6. _____

7. _____

8. _____

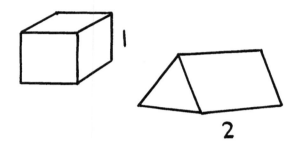

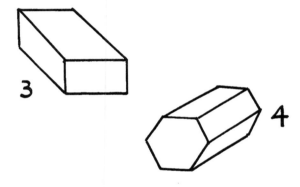

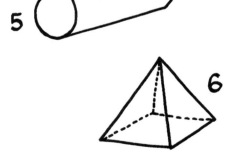

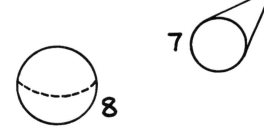

Middle Grade Book of Math Tests

Write the name of a space figure to match each description.

9. 8 vertices and 6 square faces _____

✓ sphere
✓ pyramid
✓ cone
✓ cube
✓ cylinder
✓ rectangular prism
✓ pentagonal prism
✓ triangular prism

10. 1 vertex and 1 circular face _____

11. 2 circular faces, and no vertices _____

12. no edges, and no vertices _____

13. 5 vertices,
    4 triangular faces,
    and 1 square face _____

14. 6 rectangular faces, 8 vertices, and 12 edges _____

15. 2 triangular faces, 3 rectangular faces, and 6 vertices _____

16. 2 pentagonal faces, 10 vertices, and 5 rectangular faces _____

_____ 17. How many edges are there on a cube?

_____ 18. How many edges are there on a sphere?

_____ 19. How many edges are there on a triangular prism?

_____ 20. How many faces are there on a pyramid whose base is a square?

Name _____

95

Match the formulas for volume with the correct figure.

Write each formula.

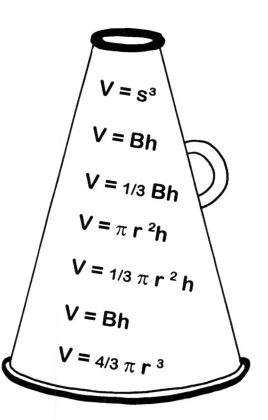

21. cube　　　　V = _____

22. sphere　　　V = _____

23. pyramid　　 V = _____

24. cylinder　　V = _____

25. cone　　　　V = _____

26. rectangular prism　V = _____

27. triangular prism　　V = _____

The figure shows formulas:

$V = s^3$

$V = Bh$

$V = 1/3\, Bh$

$V = \pi r^2 h$

$V = 1/3\, \pi r^2 h$

$V = Bh$

$V = 4/3\, \pi r^3$

Leroy is making a target for archery practice.

The front of the target has a 30-inch diameter. The target will be 10 inches thick.

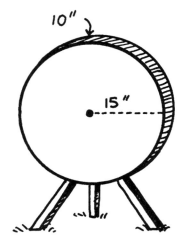

28. What space figure is this target?

　　_____

29. What is the surface area of the front surface?

　　A = _____

30. Leroy will stuff the target with straw. What is the volume of straw he will need?

　　V = _____

Choose a formula to find the volume of each space figure below. Write the formula.
Then find the volume.

31.

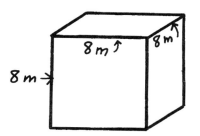

Formula: _____

V = _____

32.

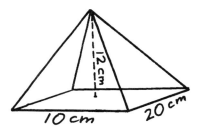

Formula: _____

V = _____

33.

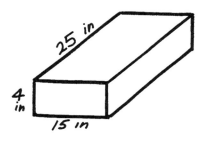

Formula: _____

V = _____

34.

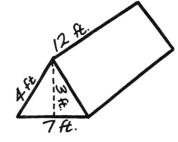

Formula: _____

V = _____

35. The ends of Chichi's barbell are a bit
uneven in size. What is the difference
between the volumes of the two spheres?

Answer: _____

36. Compare the amount of air in Spike's soccer ball with the amount of air in Leroy's basketball.

What is the difference between the two amounts?

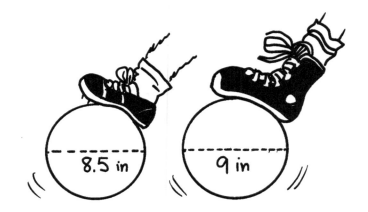

Answer: _____

37. Two friends each bought a drink at the snack bar during the ball game. Spike bought a cola drink, and Leroy bought an orange drink.

Both cans of drinks were full to the very top. Each paid $1.00 for the drink they got.

Use the measurements of the two drinks shown to find out who got the most for his money.

_____

38. Popcorn comes in two sizes of containers. How much more popcorn (volume) will fit into the large container than will fit into the small container?

Answer: _____

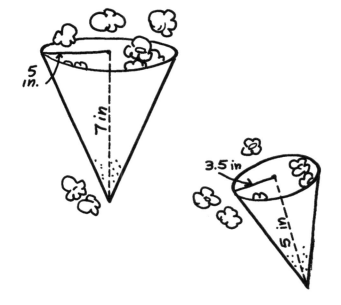

39. A group of campers pitched two tents. One was an ordinary tent in a triangular prism shape. The other was a dome tent that was exactly half of a sphere.

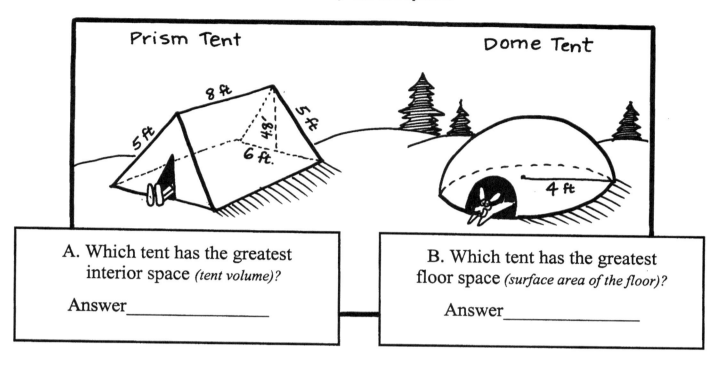

A. Which tent has the greatest interior space *(tent volume)?*

Answer_____

B. Which tent has the greatest floor space *(surface area of the floor)?*

Answer_____

40. All three boxes are full to the top. Which box holds the greatest volume of snacks? Circle the right letter.

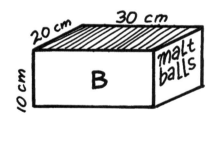

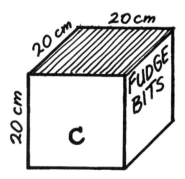

Middle Grade Book of Math Tests

MEASUREMENT

Name _____   Possible Correct Answers: 90

Date _____   Your Correct Answers: _____

For items 1–20, tell what each unit measures.

Write **length** **weight** **capacity** **time** or **temperature** next to each unit.

50 yd. Dash

_____ 1. kilogram   _____ 11. cubic liter

_____ 2. liter   _____ 12. foot

_____ 3. milliliter   _____ 13. quart

_____ 4. kilometer   _____ 14. ton

_____ 5. decade   _____ 15. cubic centimeter

_____ 6. yard   _____ 16. mile

_____ 7. gram   _____ 17. gallon

_____ 8. centimeter   _____ 18. degree

_____ 9. millimeter   _____ 19. century

_____ 10. meter   _____ 20. decimeter

21. A liter is closest to
- a. a cup
- d. a pint
- b. a gallon
- e. a quart
- c. a teaspoon
- f. a tablespoon

22. A kilogram is closest to
- a. 1 foot
- e. 1 yard
- b. 1 mile
- f. 1 pound
- c. 10 grams
- g. 1 ounce
- d. 1000 grams
- h. 10 grams

23. A kilometer is closest to
- a. a meter
- d. a yard
- b. a mile
- e. a foot
- c. an inch
- f. an acre

For items 24–31, write **>**, **<**, or **=**.

24. 14 qt _____ 3 gal

25. 40 liters _____ 10 quarts

26. 15 yd _____ 600 in

27. 2 miles _____ 12,000 feet

28. 10,000 m _____ 1 km

29. 1 ton _____ 3000 pounds

30. 1000 mg _____ 1 g

31. 3 months _____ 12 weeks

32. Which object would be about 30 centimeters wide?
- a. a doorknob
- b. a bed
- c. a dictionary
- d. a crayon

33. Which object would weigh about 15 kilograms?
- a. a train
- b. a full backpack
- c. a basketball
- d. a large bear

34. Which object would hold about 10 liters of water?
- a. a small thermos jug
- b. an Olympic-size swimming pool
- c. a birdbath

Name _____

Middle Grade Book of Math Tests

35. Which measurement is the most reasonable?
    a. The weight of an adult weight lifter: 100 kilograms
    b. The length of a fingernail: 1 meter
    c. The amount of soda pop in a can: 500 liters
    d. The weight of a paper clip: 50 grams
    e. The distance from Seattle to New York City: 10,000 kilometers

Choose the unit that would be best for finding each measurement described.

36. the amount of water in a bathtub
    a. cups
    b. square inches
    c. liters
    d. tons

37. the volume of a freezer
    a. grams
    b. ounces
    c. square millimeters
    d. cubic feet

38. the distance between two cities
    a. square inches
    b. liters
    c. cubic feet
    d. kilometers

39. the weight of 100 apples
    a. kilograms
    b. ounces
    c. tons
    d. liters

40. the area of a basketball court
    a. liters
    b. kilometers
    c. square inches
    d. square meters

Choose the tool that would be best to use for finding each measurement described.

41. the length of a movie
    a. a scale
    b. a clock
    c. a protractor
    d. a thermometer

42. the size of an angle
    a. a stopwatch
    b. a yardstick
    c. a protractor
    d. a thermometer

43. the change in temperature during a 24-hour period
    a. a scale
    b. a stopwatch
    c. a thermometer
    d. a calendar

44. the distance someone could spit a cherry seed
    a. a meter stick
    b. an inch ruler
    c. a gallon container
    d. a scale

Fill in each blank with the correct amount for changing one measurement into another.

45. The ski run was 2000 meters. How many kilometer(s)? _____

46. A snow boarder drank 3 liters of sport drink. How many milliliters? _____

47. A tennis bag weighs 5000 grams. How many kilograms? _____

48. The coach stood 150 centimeters from the sidelines. How many meters?_____

49. The new racquet weighed 70,000 milligrams. How many grams? _____

50. The race was over in 7.5 minutes. How many seconds? _____

51. Spike's favorite race has a 12-decade history. How many years? _____

52. A runner's clothing weighs 3.75 pounds. How many ounces? _____

53. The third skier fell down after skiing 47 yards. How many feet? _____

54. After a warm-up run of 4 miles, the competitors were ready. How many feet ? _____

55. One group of hockey fans drank 17 quarts of hot chocolate. How many cups? _____

56. Water covered 18 square feet of the rink's surface. How many square yards? _____

57. The water jug at the finish line held 10 gallons. How many pints? _____

58. Travel time to the ski race was 13 hours. How many minutes? _____

59. The final race is in 7 weeks. How many days? _____

60. The season is over in 9 days. How many hours? _____

Name _____

You will need a ruler that measures centimeters *and* inches for problems 61–64.

61. Measure the length in inches.
(Round to the nearest half inch.)

Answer: _____

62. Measure the length in centimeters.
(Round to the nearest whole centimeter.)

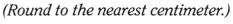

Answer: _____

63. Measure with centimeters to find the perimeter.
(Round to the nearest centimeter.)

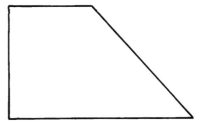

P = _____

64. Measure with inches to find the perimeter.
(Round to the nearest inch.)

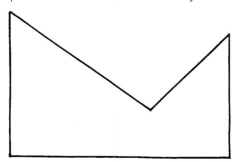

P = _____

Find the perimeter of these pools.

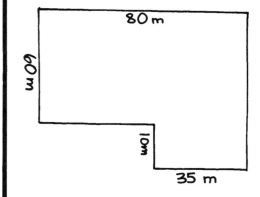

65. P = _____

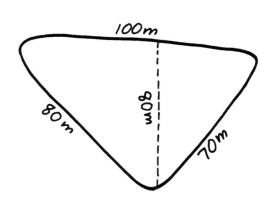

66. P = _____

Middle Grade Book of Math Tests

Copyright ©2001 by Incentive Publications, Inc., Nashville, TN.

67. A speed skater skates around the outside edge of this rink 200 times during every practice. About how much distance does she travel during these practices?

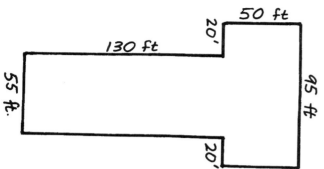

a. 550 ft^2
b. 55,000 ft
c. 110,000 ft
d. 17,100 ft^2
e. 110,000 ft^2
f. none of these

68. To warm up, the wrestlers jog around the outside of the mat before beginning their match. If they circle the mat 15 times, about how far have they traveled?

a. 953.85 m
b. 423.9 m
c. 28.26 m
d. 423.9 m^2
e. 20.25 m
f. 63.59 m
g. none of these

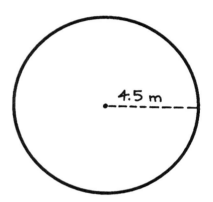
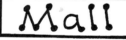

Use an inch ruler and the map scale to answer questions 69–70. Measure between the dots which represent the doors to the shops.

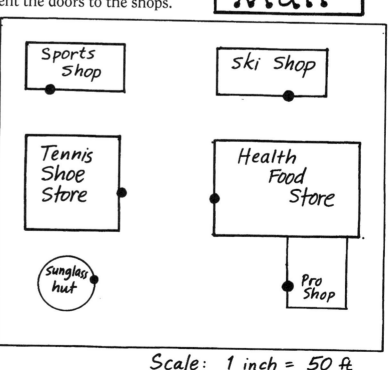

69. About how far is it from the Sports Shop to the Pro Shop?
a. 35 ft
b. 70 ft
c. 175 ft
d. 125 ft

70. About how far is it from Sunglass Hut to the Health Food Store?
a. 4 ft
b. 15 ft
c. 50 ft
d. 75 ft

Name _____

Middle Grade Book of Math Tests

You will need a ruler that measures centimeters *and* inches for problems 71–72 and 75.

71. Measure with centimeters to find the area. (Round to the nearest centimeter.)

A = _____

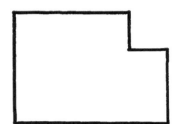

72. Measure with inches to find the area. (Round to the nearest inch.)

A = _____

Find the area of each gymnastics mat.

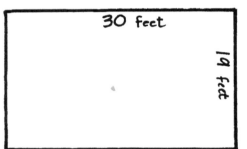

30 feet

19 feet

73. A = _____

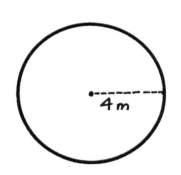

4 m

74. A = _____

75. Measure with inches to find the volume of this figure.

V = _____

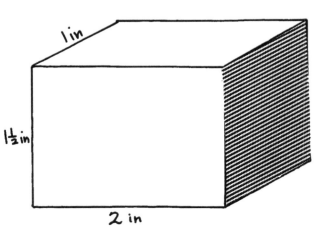

1 in

1½ in

2 in

Find the volume of each container.

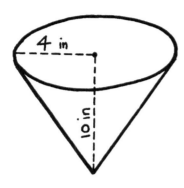

76. V = _____

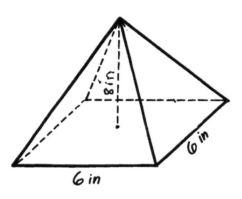

77. V = _____

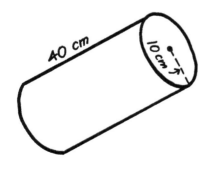

78. V = _____

79. A diving pool is 12 meters long,
6 meters wide, and 5 meters deep.
What is its capacity for holding
water? (*1 cubic meter = 1000 liters*)

Answer:_____liters

80. The new soccer uniforms will be
shipped in a box. Each uniform,
when folded, takes up 35 cubic
inches of space. Can 100 uniforms
be shipped in a box that measures
15 x 15 x 15 inches?

Answer: **yes   no**

81. A cylindrical drum
has a volume of 3140 in^3.
The radius is 10 inches.
What is the height of the cylinder?

Answer:_____

Name

Middle Grade Book of Math Tests

82. At the beginning of a soccer game, the players and fans were wearing short-sleeved or sleeveless shirts. During the soccer game, the sun went behind clouds and the temperature dropped about 20°. Most of the players and fans put on sweatshirts. After the change, the temperature was probably about

    a. 15° F   b. 85° F   c. 30° F   d. 55° F

83. The second soccer game begins at 3:15 P.M. The clock tells the current time (A.M.). How long must the players wait until the game begins?

    a. 38 minutes

    b. 138 minutes

    c. 158 minutes

    d. 108 minutes

    e. none of these

84. What time is 5 hours and 45 minutes earlier than the time shown on this clock?

Answer:_____

85. What time will it be in 9 hours and 30 minutes?

Answer:_____

86. Estimate the measurements of the angles. Which angle is . . .

    _____ a. . . . about 100°?

    _____ b. . . . about 45°?

    _____ c. . . . about 160°?

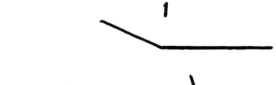

87

On Spike's map of the bike race course, 2 inches represents 1.5 miles. Spike will follow a path that goes south 9 inches, then turns southeast 4 inches, then continues west for 7 inches. How long is this path?

Answer_____

88

Leroy's backpack contains these items with these weights:

a water bottle -- 1.5 kilograms

a sweatshirt -- 400 grams

a bike repair kit -- 0.9 kilograms

a hat -- 200 grams

What is the total weight of the pack's contents?

Answer_____

89

5 soccer players practice alone each day. These are the amounts of time they practice:

1 hour, 35 minutes

1 hour, 10 minutes

75 minutes

55 minutes

1 hour, 30 minutes

What is the average length of a practice?

Answer_____

90

A powder is used to mix the sports drink for the team. The directions say to mix 1 ½ cups of powder to each quart of water. The team will drink 9 gallons. How much powder is needed?

Answer_____

Middle Grade Book of Math Tests

Graphing, Statistics, & Probability Skills Checklists

Graphing, Statistics, & Probability Test #1:

COORDINATE GRAPHING

Test Location: pages 112–117

Skill	*Test Items*
Find objects located on a two-quadrant coordinate grid	1–5
Write the coordinates of objects on a two-quadrant coordinate grid	6–10, 11–17
Place items at a given location on a two-quadrant coordinate grid	18–24
Find objects located on a four-quadrant coordinate grid	25–28, 33
Write the coordinates of objects on a four-quadrant coordinate grid	29–32
Place items at a given location on a four-quadrant coordinate grid	34–43
Plot points on a four-quadrant grid to create a graphic or illustration	44–53
Draw transformations of geometric shapes on a four-quadrant grid	54, 55

Graphing, Statistics, & Probability Test #2:

PROBABILITY

Test Location: pages 118–123

Skill	*Test Items*
Find the number of possible outcomes of events	1–5
Describe the likelihood of an event occurring	6–10
Describe all the possible outcomes of an event	11
Find the probability of an event	12–37, 54
Identify possible combinations of sets within a larger set	38, 39, 55
Identify the number of permutations for an event	40
Find the probability of two independent events	41–45
Find the probability of two dependent events	46–48
Find odds in favor and odds against an event	49–51
Use random sampling to make probability predictions	52, 53

110

Graphing, Statistics, & Probability Test #3:

STATISTICS & GRAPHING

Test Location: pages 124–133

Skill	Test Items
Recognize and define terms related to statistics	1–8
Read and interpret frequency tables	9–17
Use tables of data to solve problems	9–17, 18–40
Analyze data to find mean	18, 35, 36, 38–40
Analyze data to find range, median, and mode	19, 20, 23–34
Solve problems with data found on tables	12, 13, 14, 16, 17, 21, 22, 35–40
Read and interpret a circle graph	41–46
Read and interpret a line graph	47–51
Read and interpret a multiple line graph	52–56
Read and interpret a bar graph	57–61
Read and interpret a double bar graph	62–65
Solve problems from data shown on graphs	41–46, 49, 51, 55, 56, 58–61, 62–65

COORDINATE GRAPHING

Name _____

Date _____

Possible Correct Answers: 55

Your Correct Answers: _____

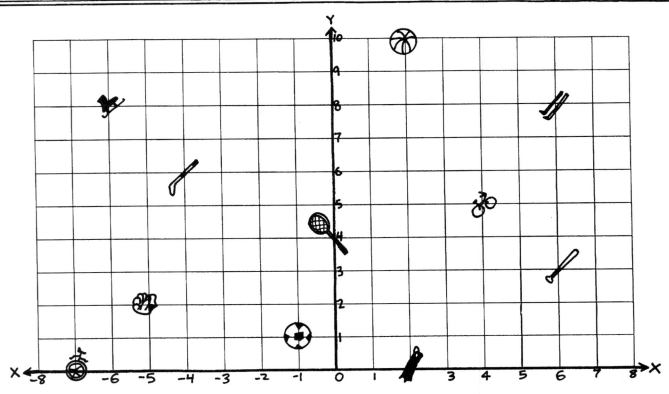

The floor in Spike's garage is littered with his sports equipment. Use the grid to locate the things he has dropped around the garage.

Write the name of the item found at each of these locations on the grid.

1. (4, 5) _____

2. (–5, 2) _____

3. (–6, 8) _____

4. (2, 10) _____

5. (–1, 1) _____

Write the coordinates of each of these items.

6. unicycle _____

7. tennis racquet _____

8. swim fin _____

9. hockey stick _____

10. skis _____

Middle Grade Book of Math Tests

A dart-throwing contest has begun. Use the grid below for questions 11–24.

Where have darts landed?
Write the coordinates to show
the location of each dart.

11. Dart A _____

12. Dart B _____

13. Dart C _____

14. Dart D _____

15. Dart E _____

16. Dart F _____

17. Dart G _____

Draw a dart at each of these coordinates.
Label each dart with its letter.

18. Draw Dart M at (–7, 9).

19. Draw Dart N at (–3, 7).

20. Draw Dart O at (3, 8).

21. Draw Dart P at (2, 0).

22. Draw Dart Q at (5, 10).

23. Draw Dart R at (–2, 12).

24. Draw Dart S at (0, 4).

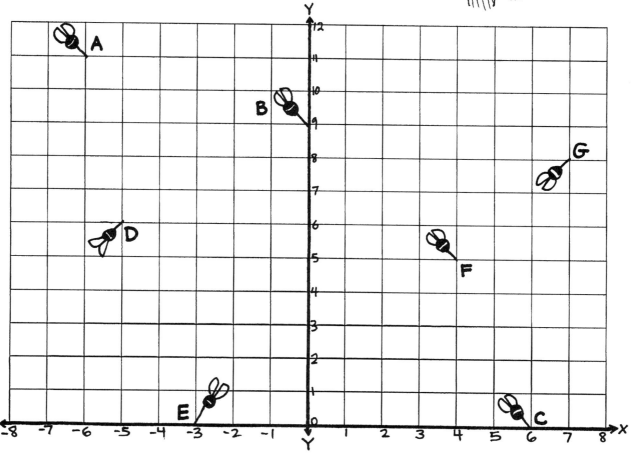

Name _____

113

Competitors are practicing for a softball-throwing contest. Where have they landed?
Use the grid to solve problems 25–33.

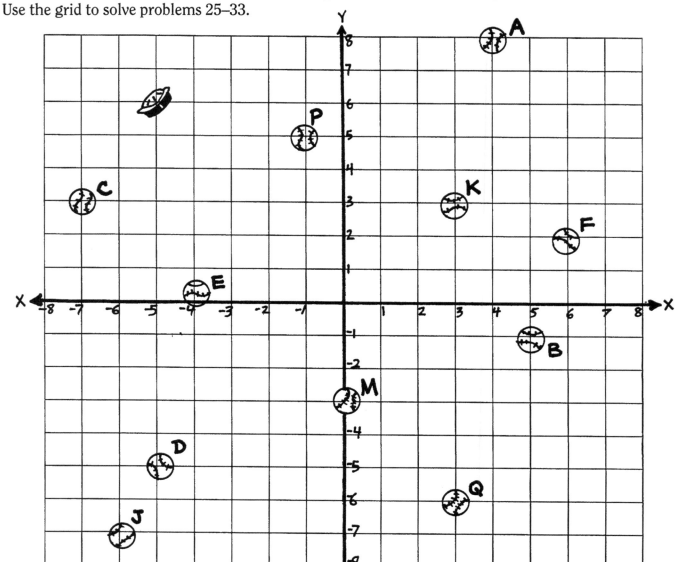

Which softball is at . . .

25. (5, –1) _____

26. (4, 8) _____

27. (0, –3) _____

28. (–1, 5) _____

Write the coordinates of . . .

29. D _____

30. Q _____

31. K _____

32. C _____

33. Someone threw a pie instead of a softball. Where did it land? _____

Name _____

Middle Grade Book of Math Tests

Use the sky grid for problems 34–43.

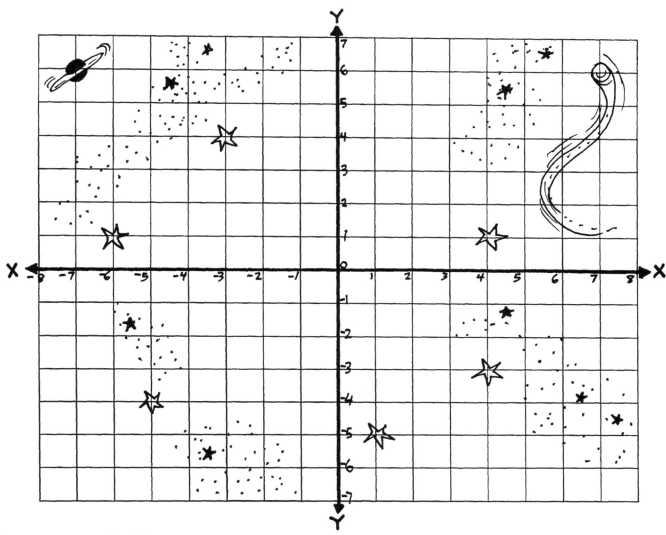

Draw a star at each of these locations:

34. (5, –6)

37. (8, 7)

40. (–4, 2)

35. (3, 0)

38. (–4, 0)

41. (3, –3)

36. (–1, 6)

39. (–8, –3)

42. (2, 5)

43. Draw a comet with the head at (–1, –2) and a tail that ends at (–6, –7).

Name _____

Copyright ©2001 by Incentive Publications, Inc., Nashville, TN.

Middle Grade Book of Math Tests

44–53. Leroy will skate a path through the obstacle course to the finish line.
Plot a point at each location shown below. Then connect the points to show the path.
(This task, done correctly, is worth 10 points.)

Plot the points shown. Then connect them in order.

A (–7, –6)	F (4, –7)	K (6, 0)	P (4, 5)	U (–8, 5)
B (–4, –6)	G (6, –7)	L (1, 1)	Q (3, 6)	V (–2, 7)
C (–5, –3)	H (6, –5)	M (1, 3)	R (–3, 4)	W (9, 8)
D (–3, –4)	I (4, –3)	N (4, 2)	S (–4, 2)	
E (–2, –2)	J (8, –1)	O (8, 6)	T (–7, 2)	

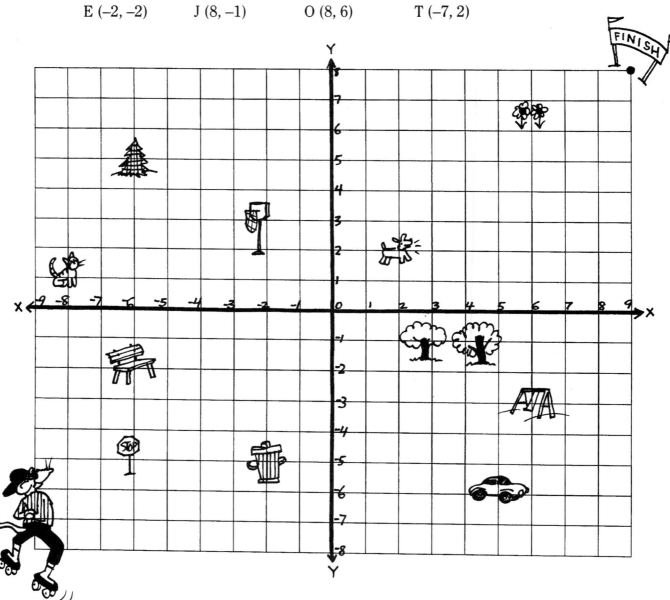

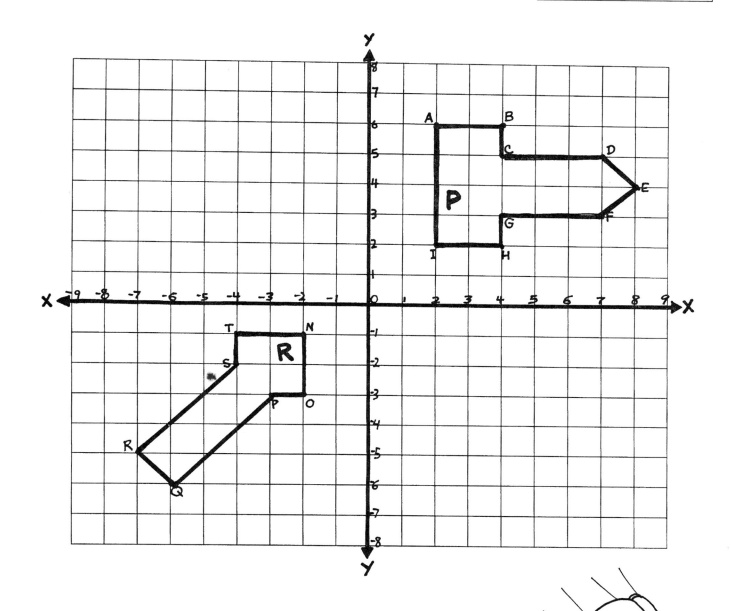

54. Draw a FLIP of Shape P on the grid. Draw the flip so that
    the point corresponding to A falls at (–2, 6).

55. You will be drawing a SLIDE of Shape R on the grid.
    Move the shape five spaces to the right and one space
    down. Draw the shape in its new position.

Name _____

Middle Grade Book of Math Tests

PROBABILITY

Name _____   Possible Correct Answers: 55

Date _____   Your Correct Answers: _____

How many different outcomes are possible for each event?

_____ 1. the flip of one coin

_____ 2. the toss of one die (6 sides)

_____ 3. the flip of two coins

_____ 4. randomly choosing a month that begins with J

_____ 5. an August birth date will have a 2
            as one of its digits *(not including the year)*

If you spin this spinner once . . .

6. How many different colors are possible outcomes? _____

7. Which color is most likely? _____

8. Which color is least likely? _____

9. Which colors are equally likely? _____

_____

10. Which color is less likely than blue? _____

11. You flip a coin three times. What are all the possible outcomes of those three events?
    Write them. Use H for heads and T for tails.

_____

Write the answers to questions 12–15 as **0**, **1**, or any ratio in between.

What is the probability that . . .

_____ 12. the toss of two coins will result in 2 heads?

_____ 13. two odd numbers will have an even sum?

_____ 14. a randomly-chosen day will begin with the letter S?

_____ 15. the toss of one die will result in an even number?

Some skateboarders will spin to see which trick they must perform.
Notice the code letters to match each trick.
Write a ratio to show each probability described.

_____16. P (K)

_____17. P (S)

_____18. P (S or B)

_____19. P (not K)

_____20. P (N, T, or I)

Spike spins this spinner once.

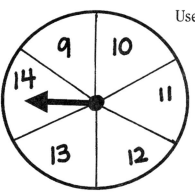

Use a ratio to show the probability for each outcome.

_____ 21. P (an odd number)

_____ 22. P (an even number > 10)

_____ 23. P (a number divisible by 5)

_____ 24. P (a number divisible by 3)

_____ 25. P (a number < 14)

Name _____

Middle Grade Book of Math Tests

48 bikers are competing in an international race.

16 are from the United States

12 are from Canada

9 are from Mexico

7 are from Japan

4 are from France

A biker's name is drawn from the registration list.
What is the probability that . . .

_____ 26. the biker is not from the United States?

_____ 27. the biker is from France or Japan?

_____ 28. the biker is from Mexico?

_____ 29. the biker is not from Canada?

_____ 30. the biker is from Japan or Mexico?

_____ 31. the biker is from North or Central America?

The socks in Leroy's sock drawer are bundled together in pairs. Leroy rushes to his drawer to grab some socks for the race. He reaches in and grabs a pair without looking.

Write a ratio to show the probability of each event.

_____ 32. P (b)   _____ 34. P (g or r)   _____ 36. P (not b)

_____ 33. P (not w)   _____ 35. P (g)   _____ 37. P (r or w)

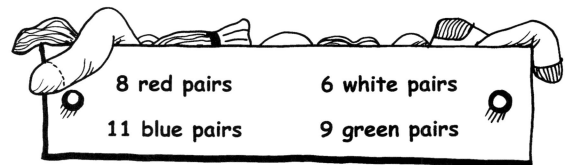

8 red pairs   6 white pairs

11 blue pairs   9 green pairs

Leroy's Sock Drawer

38. 6 scuba divers are getting ready for a dive. For safety, they always dive in pairs.

What are the possible pairs they could form? Use the first letter of each name as you write all the pairs.

_____

_____

Scuba Divers
Spike
Buddy
Penny
Rufus
Leroy
J.J.

39. Leroy has a special talent for fashion when he dives. Today he is trying to get just the right combination of colors for his wetsuit and swim fins.

Wet Suits
magenta *(m)*
yellow *(y)*
chartreuse *(c)*
ruby red *(r)*

Swim Fins
turquoise *(t)*
fuchsia *(f)*
orange *(o)*
black *(b)*

These are his choices.

What are the possible combinations he might choose? List them here.
Use the first letter of each color as you write the pairs.

40. Four swimmers are in line to rent wetsuits. They are: Roxie, Moxie, Bud, and Mitch. How many different permutations are possible for their arrangement in line? (That is, how many different possibilities are there for their order in line?)

Answer: _____

Leroy flips a coin to see which of two bulls he will ride. Then, he draws a number (1–5) to learn where he will fall in the order of the riders.
He is the first to toss and draw.
What is the probability that he will get . . .

_____ 41. heads and # 1?

_____ 42. heads and a # < 5?

_____ 43. tails and a #2 or #3?

_____ 44. tails and 5th place?

_____ 45. tails and neither # 1 nor #5?

A pen of bulls has 8 black bulls, 4 brown bulls, and 6 white bulls.
Riders are randomly assigned one of the 18 bulls.
A bull will not be ridden more than once.

_____ 46. What is the probability that the first rider will get a black bull?

_____ 47. If the first rider gets a black bull, what is the probability that the second rider will be assigned a white bull?

_____ 48. What is the probability that the first and second riders each get a white bull?

In addition to the main prizes, there are 10 bonus prize envelopes for the bull riders. Five envelopes contain $50 bills. Three contain $100 bills. Two contain $500 bills.
Leroy is the first rider to choose an envelope.

_____ 49. What are Leroy's odds in favor of getting a $100 bill?

_____ 50. What are Leroy's odds against getting a $500 bill?

_____ 51. What are Leroy's odds in favor of getting a $50 bill?

Name _____

Middle Grade Book of Math Tests

52. The rodeo doctor wanted to find out how many of the bull riders were competing today with serious injuries. There were so many competitors that he did not have time to visit all the bull riders. He sampled 30 of the 400 riders. He found that 6 out of the 30 were competing with stitches or fractures. Based on this information, he was able to predict how many such problems he might find in the whole group of 400 riders.

What would be your prediction?_____

53.
The fans at this rodeo are especially loyal to a favorite bull named *Rosie*. Sales of *Rosie* t-shirts are booming at the Rodeo Shop. A sampling of fans found that 32 out of 100 fans were wearing a *Rosie* t-shirt. How many *Rosie* t-shirts would you expect to find in the whole crowd of 1,000 fans?

Answer:_____

54. Out of the 105 bulls that can be ridden today, 50 are considered *manageable*. 35 are labeled *moderately wild*. The remaining 30 are considered, *extremely wild*.
A bull's name is drawn from a hat for the first rider.
What is the probability that this bull will be extremely wild?

Answer:_____

Outfit Design
silver streaks
gold sparkles

Boot Color
shocking yellow
fire orange
screaming green

55. Fancy Frederick is known as the bull rider who dresses with a flair. He combines dazzling outfits with outrageous boots. When he dresses for the ride today, he picks from the choices shown. How many different outfit-boot combinations could Frederick wear?

Answer:_____

STATISTICS & GRAPHING

Name _____

Possible Correct Answers: 65

Date _____

Your Correct Answers: _____

Choose the matching term for each definition.

a. data	_____	1. average of a number of data items
b. median	_____	2. information given in numerical form
c. statistics	_____	3. number of times an item appears in a set of data
d. frequency	_____	4. collection, organization, and use of sets of numerical data
e. mode	_____	5. number that appears most frequently in a set of data
f. line graph	_____	6. difference between the greatest and least numbers in a set of data
g. mean	_____	7. a graph that uses lines to show changes in data over time
h. range	_____	8. number that falls in the middle of a set of data arranged in order

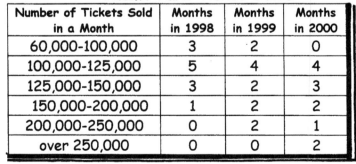

Theme Park Ticket Sales

Number of Tickets Sold in a Month	Months in 1998	Months in 1999	Months in 2000
60,000-100,000	3	2	0
100,000-125,000	5	4	4
125,000-150,000	3	2	3
150,000-200,000	1	2	2
200,000-250,000	0	2	1
over 250,000	0	0	2

9. Did total ticket sales generally increase or decrease from 1998–2000? _____

10. Over $\frac{1}{3}$ of the total months for 3 years fell into which range of ticket sales? _____

11. How many months in 1999 had sales of 150,000 or fewer tickets? _____

12. About how many tickets were sold in 1998?
 a. 1,205,000 – 1,575,000   b. 120,500 – 152,500   c. 1,500,000 – 2,000,000

AGES of VISITORS
to Extreme Thrills Theme Park

Age Groupings	Number of Visitors in 1999	Number of Visitors in 2000
Pre-School (0-5)	16,900	28,010
Primary School (6-10)	378,808	350,660
Middle School (11-13)	411,101	498,900
High School (14-18)	342,000	348,000
Ages 19-25	200,900	201,150
Ages 26-40	475,000	424,890
Ages 41-50	316,090	277,888
Ages 51-65	82,777	92,190
Ages 65-75	12,471	31,200
over 75	8,970	19,850

13. Which 2 age groups together totaled about 850,000 in 2000?

_____ and

_____

14. Which 2 age groups more than doubled in attendance between 1999 and 2000?

_____ and

_____

15. How many age groups showed smaller attendance in 2000 than in 1999?

_____

16. Which over-18 age group had the strongest attendance over the 2-year period?

_____

17. Which number is the closest estimate of the total number of visitors attending the park in 2000?

    a. 2,000,000   b. 2,250,000   c. 2,100,000   d. 2,500,000

Name

125

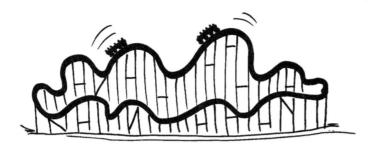

Theme Park Attractions

Lengths of Rides or Events

Type of Attraction	Average Length in Minutes
Roller coasters	7
Spinning Rides	4.5
Children's Rides	11.5
Theme Trips	14
Water Rides	9
Walking Events	12.5
Extreme Thrills Events	25

18. What is the mean (average) length of a ride or event? Round to the nearest tenth.

_____

19. What is the range of lengths of rides or events?

_____

20. What is the median of the statistics provided on the table?

_____

21. If a visitor to the park rides or takes part in one of each kind of event, with an hour to walk to and wait for each, approximately how much time will that take?

Answer:
approximately _____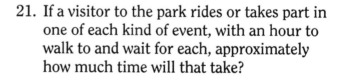

22. Approximately how long would it take a visitor to ride 6 different roller coasters, if the walk between coasters and the waiting time averages 40 minutes for each?

Answer:
approximately _____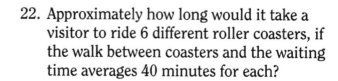

Name _____

Middle Grade Book of Math Tests

100 high school students were asked to vote for the best event in each of four categories. The tables show their votes. Give the range, median, and mode for each set of statistics.

ROLLER COASTERS	
Name of Coaster	Number of Votes
The Terminator	19
Black Widow	11
Scream Machine	9
Tiger's Tail	3
Shockwave	4
Steel Demon	4
Cannonball	3
Triple Terrible Loop	8
The Outlaw	4
Mean Streak	26
Abomination	9

ROLLER COASTERS

23. range _____

24. median _____

25. mode _____

SPINNING RIDES

26. range _____

27. median _____

28. mode _____

SPINNING RIDES	
Name of Ride	Number of Votes
Stomach Cruncher	12
Topsy-Turvy	9
The Tornado	16
Revolution	13
Circle-Mania	9
Tummy Twister	9
The Scrambler	14
Zig-Zag Zombie	9
Nausea	9

WATER RIDES	
Name of Ride	Number of Votes
Tidal Wave	12
Raging River	17
Ocean Rampage	32
Tsunami	8
The Last River	2
Angry River	10
Desperate Falls	12
The Lost Submarine	7

WATER RIDES

29. range _____

30. median _____

31. mode _____

EXTREME THRILLS

32. range _____

33. median _____

34. mode _____

EXTREME THRILLS	
Name of Attraction	Number of Votes
The Plunge	8
Danger Drop	2
Bridge Bungee	2
Sky Surfer	52
The Air Walker	5
Cliff Hanger	21

Name _____

127

Tossing ping-pong balls into jars is a favorite game for this group of friends. They like trying to toss the balls into the jars!
It is not as easy as it looks.

5 balls are tossed in each game. Different jars have different point values. The table shows the points each player earned in each game.

Use the data in the chart
to answer the questions.

SCORES FOR PING-PONG BALL TOSS

	Game 1	Game 2	Game 3	Game 4	Game 5
Spike	30	85	15	25	30
Chichi	40	55	84	30	10
Max	75	35	40	55	10
Rufus	100	0	65	45	25
Leroy	70	35	30	40	70
J.J.	15	25	35	15	35

35. What was the mean (average) score for all players in Game 3? _____

36. What was the mean (average) score for all players in Game 5? _____

37. Which game had the highest average score? _____

38. What was Spike's average score for a game? _____

39. What was Max's average score for a game? _____

40. A prize was given for any player who averaged more than 40 points a game over the 5-game stretch. Which players did NOT win a prize?

Name _____

Middle Grade Book of Math Tests

The circle graph gives information about the categories of visitors who visited the Extreme Thrills Theme Park over the past weekend.

Use the graph to answer the questions below. (The numbers shown on the graph represent a count of individual visitors.)

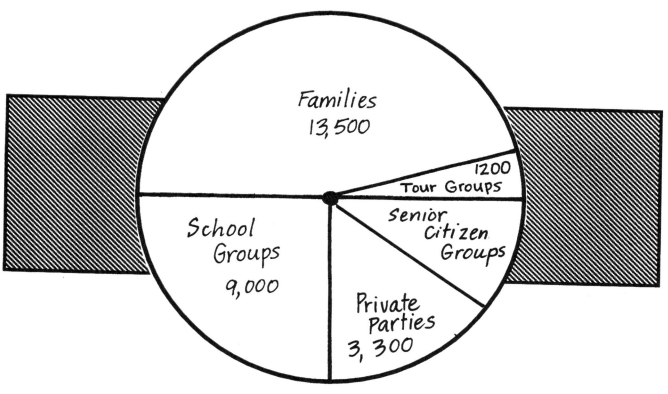

41. Which group represents about 25% of the total visitors? _____

42. Which group made up about 20% less of the total than the private parties? _____

43. Which group comprised 45% of the total? _____

44. The total number of visitors last weekend was 30,000.
    How many visitors came with senior citizen groups? _____

45. 25% of the people in the tour groups
    came from Germany. How many people is this? _____

46. How many more visitors came with school groups than with private parties? _____

Middle Grade Book of Math Tests

This graph shows the number of injuries reported at the theme park during the week.

47. Which 3-day period had the smallest number of injuries?

_____

48. About how many fewer injuries were reported on Sunday than on Saturday?

    a. about 40

    b. about 65

    c. about 55

    d. about 75

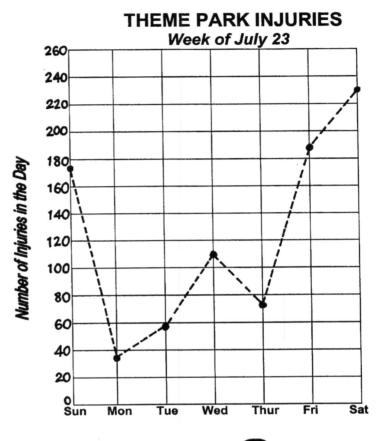

THEME PARK INJURIES
Week of July 23

49. 10% of Friday's injuries were related to sunburn or heatstroke.
About how many was this?

_____

50. Which day had 120 more injuries than Wednesday?

_____

51. About how many injuries were reported all together during the week?

    a. 900   b. 1000   c. 700   d. 600

Three of the first attractions offered in the Extreme Thrills part of the park were skydiving, bungee jumping, and white water kayaking. The graph shows the 7-year history of the numbers of visitors who tried each of these sports.

Use the graph to answer the questions below.

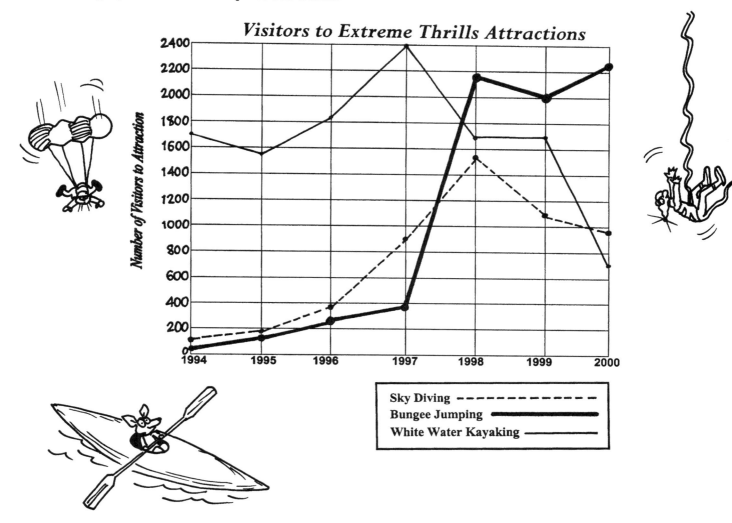

52. Which sport had the greatest change (gain or loss) from 1994 to 2000? _____

53. About how many visitors did bungee jumping gain from 1997 to 1998? _____

54. Which sport showed a drop of over 1000 visitors during a 3-year period? _____

55. What is the difference between the highest and lowest participation in bungee jumping?

_____

56. How many visitors did sky diving gain between 1995 and 1998? _____

Name _____

Middle Grade Book of Math Tests

Use the bar graph below to answer the questions about the money taken in last week at some of the theme park's great eating spots.

Week's Restaurant Revenues

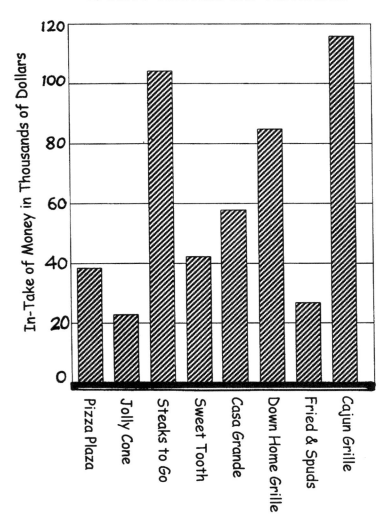

57. How many restaurants took in more money than the Sweet Tooth?

_____

58. Which food spot took in about $20,000 less than Steaks to Go?

_____

59. About how much money was taken all together at the Cajun and Down Home Grilles?

_____

60. Which food spot took in about $20,000 more than the Pizza Palace?

_____

61. About how much was collected all together from these restaurants during the week?

    a. $350,000   b. $490,000   c. $550,000   d. $400,000

Name _____

Middle Grade Book of Math Tests

Use the graph to answer questions about the kinds of food customers choose to eat at the theme park. Notice that the graph shows the average number of customers choosing a kind of food daily both during the daytime and after 6:00 p.m.

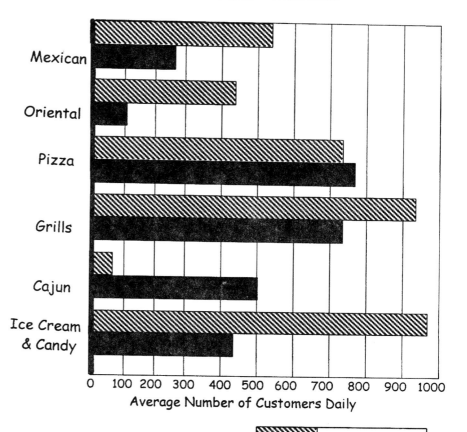

Customer Choices

Average Number of Customers Daily

| | Daytime |
| | Evening (after 6 pm) |

62. The average customer spends $8 on pizza.
About how much money will the pizza places collect in an average day (day and evening combined)?

    a. $6400   b. $120,000   c. $64,000   d. $12,000

63. How many more customers choose ice cream & candy during the day than at night?

    a. about 520   b. about 600   c. about 400   d. about 700

64. Which kind of food attracts about 250 fewer customers in the evening than Cajun? _____

65. About how many more customers choose food at the grills rather than at the Oriental restaurants (day and evening combined)?

    a. 1700   b. 1200   c. 600   d. 800

Name _____

Middle Grade Book of Math Tests

Pre-Algebra Skills Checklists

Pre-Algebra Test # 1:

INTEGERS

Test Location: pages 136–141

Skill	Test Items
Identify the opposite value of a real number	1–5
Identify the absolute value of a real number	6–8
Compare integers	9–14
Order integers	15
Add integers	16–19
Subtract integers	20–23
Multiply integers	24, 26, 27, 31
Divide integers	25, 28–30
Estimate the answer to a problem with integers	32, 33, 43–44
Solve problems with multiple operations with integers	34, 35, 38, 39, 45
Recognize the meaning of a mathematical sentence	36
Find missing numbers in integer equations	39–42
Identify a number sentence that will solve a problem	46
Solve word problems with integers	47–50

Middle Grade Book of Math Tests

Pre-Algebra Test # 2:

BEGINNING EQUATIONS

Test Location: pages 142–147

Pre-Algebra Test # 3:

EQUATIONS & INEQUALITIES

Test Location: pages 148–152

INTEGERS

Name _____   Possible Correct Answers: 50

Date _____   Your Correct Answers: _____

Do not use a calculator for any part of this test.

1. A diver sits on the deck of a boat that is 9 meters above the water's surface (+9).

   What is the opposite value of this number? _____

2. Another diver is 29 feet below the surface (−29).

   What is the opposite value of this number? _____

Write the **opposite value** for each number.	Write the **absolute value** for each number.
3. **−30** _____	6. **24.5** _____
4. **−0.05** _____	7. **−113** _____
5. **6 ½** _____	8. **$\frac{12}{7}$** _____

Write < or > in each box.

9. 150 ☐ −700

10. $-\frac{1}{2}$ ☐ − 5.5

11. −4.4 ☐ −6.9

12. 45 ☐ −145

13. −28 ☐ −3

14. $16\frac{1}{2}$ ☐ $-5\frac{1}{2}$

Middle Grade Book of Math Tests

15. Write these numbers on the flags in order from smallest to largest.

25   **–25**   **18.6**   **–18.6**   **–3**   **3**   **12**

16. Spike descended to **86.6** feet below the surface. Leroy went **3.9** feet deeper than Spike. How deep did Leroy descend?

Answer:_____

17. –7 + 93 = _____

18. 45 + -9 = _____

19. –15 + -62 = _____

20. Leroy dove from the deck of the boat **10.3** meters above the water's surface to **37.5** meters below the surface. (-37.5). What is the difference between the two locations?

Answer:_____

21. –5 – -12 = _____

22. –87 + 13 = _____

23. –100 – -60 = _____

24. Chichi went into debt $37 to buy diving equipment **(-$37)**. Spike went into 5 times the debt to buy his equipment.

What is the total amount of Spike's debt?

Answer:_____

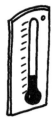 

25. The temperature on Friday was –18.5 F°. This was 5 times colder than Monday's temperature.

What was the temperature on Monday?

Answer: _____

26. **–11 x 303 =** _____

27. **26 x –4 =** _____

28. **1000 ÷ –10 =** _____

29. **–96 ÷ –4 =** _____

30. **–198 ÷ 6 =** _____

31. **–1000 x –100 =** _____

32. Estimate the answer:

(–62 x 19) + –104 = _____

a. about 1220

b. about –1220

c. about 2200

d. about –2200

33. Estimate the answer:

(1386 ÷ –99) x –7 = _____
a. about 100
b. about –100
c. about –30
d. about 30

Name _____

Middle Grade Book of Math Tests

34. Circle the correct answer.

12 + -119 – -31 + 17 =

a. -121   c. -59

b. 121   d. 59

35. Circle the correct answer.

-900 + 905 – -1800 + -90 =

a. -1715   c. 1885

b. 1715   d. 3695

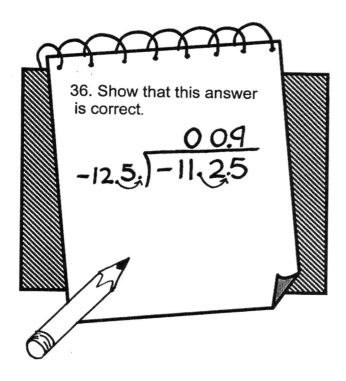

36. Show that this answer is correct.

$$-12.5\overline{)-11.25}$$ = 0 0.9

37. Which sentence represents this math statement?

17(3 – –15) =

a. seventeen and the product of three and fifteen

b. the product of seventeen and the difference between 3 and negative 15

c. seventeen times negative eighteen

d. the product of seventeen and 12

38. Which 2 problems have the same solution? (Circle the letters.)

a. **15 + 7 – -3 + -9**

b. **49 – -8 + 3 –70**

c. **(-35 + -13) ÷ 3**

d. **–2 x (16 ÷ -2)**

e. **–1000 x –3 + -10**

Middle Grade Book of Math Tests

Fill in the missing numbers.

39. **−900 +** ☐ **x 2 = −1820**

40. ☐ **x − 40 + 70 = 2070**

41. **10,000 −** ☐ **= −4700**

42. ☐ **÷ −20 = −2800**

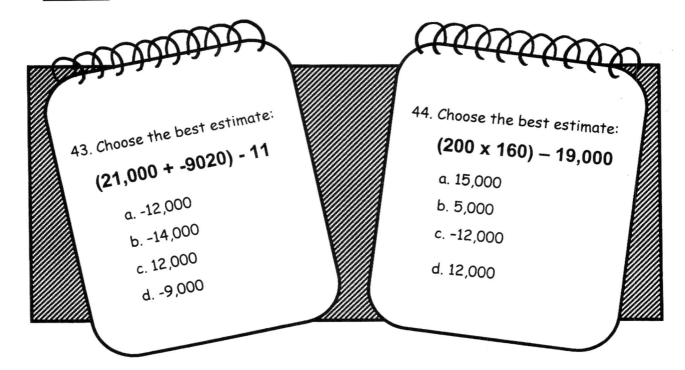

43. Choose the best estimate:

(21,000 + -9020) - 11

a. -12,000

b. -14,000

c. 12,000

d. -9,000

44. Choose the best estimate:

(200 x 160) − 19,000

a. 15,000

b. 5,000

c. -12,000

d. 12,000

45. The answer to a problem is **0**. What is the problem?

a. -20 x -30 − -600

b. (-300 + 100) ÷ 4

c. 100 ÷ -4 + -50 + 75

46. Read the following problem.

Leroy jumped from a 10.5-foot diving platform. He descended to 12.8 feet below the surface of the lake. How far did he travel all together?

Which number sentence represents the problem? *(Circle one letter.)*

a. 10.5 − 12.8 = _____

b. 10.5 − −12.8 = _____

c. 12.8 − 10.5 = _____

d. 10.5 + −12.8 = _____

47. A diver descended 115 feet (-115) below the surface. She went back 35 feet toward the surface and stopped. Where did she stop?

_____

48. The difference between two temperatures is 63.5°. One temperature is 17°. What is the other temperature?

_____

49. Saturday's temperature is –15.9°. This is 3 times colder than Friday's temperature. What was Friday's temperature? _____

50. An elevator began a trip from 5 floors below ground level. It traveled 17 floors up. At what floor did it stop?_____

BEGINNING EQUATIONS

Name _____   Possible Correct Answers: 40

Date _____   Your Correct Answers: _____

1. Player # 18 weighs less than half of Boe's weight.

   Which player is Boe? _____

112 lbs.   175 lbs.   240 lbs.   130 lbs.   200 lbs.

2. One player's number is 5 more than 3 times another player's number.

   What are the numbers of the two players? _____ and _____

3. Spike carried the ball 32 yards. His friend Leroy carried the ball ½ as many yards as Spike. Which expression represents the distance the ball was carried by Leroy?

   a. **32 + ½**

   b. **½ x 32**

   c. **32 x 2**
      2

   d. **32 – ½**

4. Which description matches this mathematical expression?

   9(40-n)

   a. the difference between a number and 40

   b. nine times the sum of a number and 40

   c. nine times the difference between 40 and a number

   d. the difference between 40 and a number divided by nine

5. Twice the weight of Joe's helmet **(h)** and uniform **(u)** together.

_____

6. Spike's weight clothed in all his football equipment **(s)** decreased by the weight of all his equipment **(e)**.

_____

7. The amount of pizza **(p)** eaten by the whole football team divided by the number of players on the team **(n)**.

_____

8. Choose the expression that shows how many fans left before the end of the game.

    1800 fans arrived before the game began.

    A number of fans arrived during the second half of the game.

    $\frac{1}{3}$ of all the fans left before the end of the game.

    a. $1800 + n - 3n$ b. $3 \times 1800 + n$ c. $1800 - 3n$ d. $(1800 + n) \div 3$

Simplify each expression below.

9. $25 b + 39 b$ _____

10. $n + n + 3n$ _____

11. $12p \div 3p + 2$ _____

12. $k + 6(3k + 2)$ _____

13. $16a + 45d - 12a$ _____

14. $4z + 10 - 9$ _____

Name _____

Middle Grade Book of Math Tests

PROPERTIES

A Associative Property

C Commutative Property

D Distributive Property

I Identity Property

Z Property of Zero

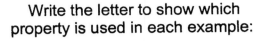

Write the letter to show which property is used in each example:

_____15. **30 x -4 = -4 x 30**

_____16. **-50 x 1 = -50**

_____17. **6(7 + 9) = (6 x 7) + (6 x 9)**

_____18. **-3 + (6 + 8) = (-3 + 6) + 8**

_____19. **-253 + 0 = -253**

Circle the equation that matches each statement.

20. Bud (b) drank 12 more cans of juice than Wally (w).

    a. $b + 12 = w$

    b. $b + w = 12$

    c. $b + w > 12$

    d. $12 - b = w$

21. Joe (j) has 45 more blisters than Leroy (l). Together they have 70 blisters.

    a. $2j - 45 = 70$

    b. $j - 45 = 70$

    c. $j + (j + 45) = 70$

    d. $2 \times 45 = j$

22. Wednesday's game (w) lasted 20 minutes more than $\frac{1}{2}$ as long as Friday's game (f).

    a. $w + f = 2$

    b. $w + 20 = f \div 2$

    c. $w = \frac{1}{2} f + 20$

    d. $f = 20 \times 2$

23. C.J. scored 48 points in the last 4 games. The number of points he scored today (n) was 7 more than the average number of those last 4 games.

    a. $n = 48 - 7$

    b. $n = 48 \div 4 + 7$

    c. $n = 48 \times 7$

    d. $n = 48 + 7$

Write an equation to match each mathematical statement.

24. During football season there were ⅓ as many sprained ankles **(a)** as there were pulled muscles **(m).**

25. Leroy's visit to the hospital for a sprained ankle **(a)** cost $30 more than Boe's visit to the doctor for a sprained wrist **(w).**

Choose the equation that will solve the problem.

26. The team practices 9 hours more in September than in October. Between the two months, they practiced 143 hours. How many hours **(h)** did they practice in October?

a. h = 143 - h

b. h + (h + 9) = 143

c. h + 9 = 143

d. 143 – h = 9

27. Leroy sat on the bench twice as long as Spike. The total time both of them spent on the bench was 69 minutes. How much time did Spike sit on the bench? **(t)?**

a. t + 2t = 69

b. 2t = 69

c. 2 x 69 = t

d. 69 – t = 2

Middle Grade Book of Math Tests

Choose an equation to solve each problem.

28. 94 snack bars were eaten by 4 football players. Max ate 12. Wally ate twice as many as Max. Spike ate 16. How many did the fourth player eat (x)?
    a. 94 x 4 = x
    b. 12 + 24 + x = 94
    c. 12 + 2x + 16 = 94
    d. x = 94 – 12 – 24 – 16

    Answer: _____

29. Team A drank 18 quarts of Energy Drink. Team B drank 12 quarts more than $\frac{1}{2}$ as much as Team A. How much did Team B drink (d)?
    a. d = 18 x 2 + 12
    b. d = (18 ÷ 2) + 12
    c. d = (18–12) ÷ 2
    d. d = 12 x 18 + 2

    Answer: _____

30. Last night's football game lasted 141 minutes. (This included time between plays.) Spike was on the field for 30 minutes more than $\frac{1}{3}$ of the game. How much time (t) did Spike spend on the field?
    a. t = (141 + 30) ÷ 3
    b. t = (141 x 3) ÷ 30
    c. t = (141 ÷ 3) + 30
    d. t = (141 ÷ 3) – 30

    Answer: _____

Simplify each equation.

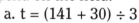

31. **x + x + 6 = 84**

33. **5x + 5 + x = -40**

32. **6(3p + 8) = 120**

34. **700 + 2n + 10 = 770**

Solve the equations.

35. $1550 = \frac{1}{4}\,n$

n =

36. $9\,(-4x) = -180$

x =

37. $18.5 + 3n = 48.5$

n =

38. $-20 - x = -75$

x =

39. Between the two of them,
Wally and Bud have played
football for 28 years.
Bud has played 4 years
longer than Wally.
How many years have they each played?

Bud_____

Wally_____

40. Al is 2 years older than twice Ed's age.
The sum of their ages is 11.
How old are they?

Al_____

Ed_____

Middle Grade Book of Math Tests

EQUATIONS & INEQUALITIES

Name _____

Possible Correct Answers: 25

Date _____

Your Correct Answers: _____

Solve these equations. Find the value of x.

1. $10 + 13x = 62$

3. $40 = \dfrac{x + 4}{9}$

2. $3x + 22 - x = 162$

4. $-360 = x + 4$

5. $3.5 + -12.5 - x = -17$

6. $x + 2x = -42$

7. Is this equation solved correctly?

$$4(x+5) = -44$$
$$4x + 20 = -44$$
$$4x = -64$$
$$x = -16$$

yes   **no**

8. Is this equation solved correctly?

$$(3+q)22 = 88$$
$$66 + 22q = 88$$
$$22q = 22$$
$$q = 1$$

yes   **no**

9.   Circle the correct equation. Then find the answer.

A baseball player ate 16 ½ pancakes for breakfast. This was 7 ¼ more pancakes than his stomach needed. How many did his stomach need?

  a. x = 16 ½ + 7 ¼

  b. x = 16 ½ ÷ 7 ¼

  c. 16 ½ - x = 7 ¼

Answer_____

10.   Circle the correct equation. Then find the answer.

14 gallons of Sports Juice was brought to the game. 4 gallons spilled. The team drank ½ of the remaining juice. How much did they drink?

  a. (14 − 4) ÷ 2 = x

  b. 14 − x = 2

  c. ½ (14 − 4) = x

Answer_____

Middle Grade Book of Math Tests

Solve each problem below.
Write the equation you used to solve the problem
next to your solution.

11. Last season, Spike's team won 9 more games than they did this season.
    Together they won 47 games in the two seasons.
    How many did they win last season?

    Equation: _____

    Solution: _____

12. The team traveled 288 miles to a game. The trip took 4.5 hours.
    What was their rate of travel in miles per hour?

    Equation: _____

    Solution: _____

13. Write an equation. Use it to solve the problem.

    On the day of Spike's first baseball game, the temperature was 58° F. This temperature was 67°
    higher than on the day of his first ski race. What was the temperature on the day of the ski race?

    Equation: _____ Solution: _____

14. The team practiced 12 hours one week, 10 hours the next week, and 14 hours the third week.
    Their average weekly practice time over 4 weeks was 11 hours. How long did they practice in the
    fourth week?

    Equation: _____ Solution: _____

Name _____

Middle Grade Book of Math Tests

For each inequality, circle the numbers that would be solutions.

15.	$x + 4 < 10$	8	–3	7	9	5
16.	$3x \geq 9$	–3	3	–4	7	0
17.	$x \leq 20$	–30	4	15	25	–9
18.	$\frac{1}{2}x < 8$	4	2	–12	40	–10

19. Which inequality is represented by the above graph?

    a. $x > -2$ c. $x \leq -2$

    b. $x > 2$ d. $x \geq -2$

20. Which inequality is represented by the above graph?

    a. $x > 3$ c. $x \leq 3$

    b. $x < 3$ d. $x \geq 3$

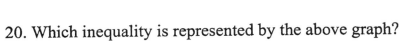

Name _____

Middle Grade Book of Math Tests

21. Two baseball teams together had 21 injuries during a tournament.

    a. If Team Green had 12 injuries,
how many injuries did Team Red have?   Answer: _____

    b. If Team Green had 16 injuries,
how many injuries did Team Red have?   Answer: _____

3x + y = 6	
x	**y**
-2	
7	
4	
-10	

y = -4x	
x	**y**
	20
	-40
	24
	-16

22. Read the equation above.
Look at the values of x.
Write the value of y for each x value.

23. Read the equation above.
Look at the values of y.
Write the value of x for each y value.

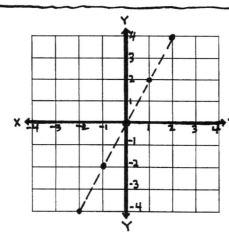

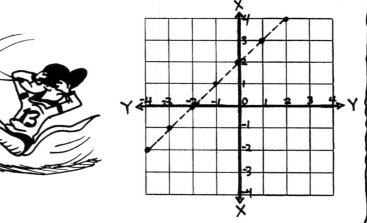

24. Which equation matches the graph?
Circle the correct equation.

    a. $2y = x$

    b. $x + y = 2$

    c. $y = 2x$

    d. $x - 2 = y$

25. Which equation matches the graph?
Circle the correct equation.

    a. $y = x + 2$

    b. $x + y = 2$

    c. $x - 3y$

    d. $x - 4 = y$

Middle Grade Book of Math Tests

KEEPING TRACK OF SKILLS

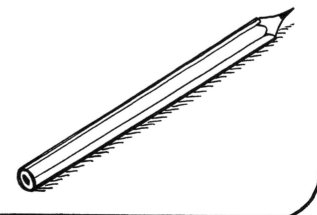

STUDENT PROGRESS RECORD — MATH SKILLS

Student Name _____

TEST DATE	NUMBERS & COMPUTATION TESTS	SCORE	COMMENTS & NEEDS
	Test # 1 Whole Number Concepts	___ of 50	
	Test # 2 Addition & Subtraction	___ of 25	
	Test # 3 Multiplication & Division	___ of 30	
	Test # 4 Mixed Operations	___ of 40	

TEST DATE	FRACTIONS & DECIMALS TESTS	SCORE	COMMENTS & NEEDS
	Test # 1 Fractions	___ of 65	
	Test # 2 Decimals	___ of 50	
	Test # 3 Fractions, Decimals, & Percents	___ of 45	
	Test # 4 Money	___ of 25	

TEST DATE	PROBLEM-SOLVING TESTS	SCORE	COMMENTS & NEEDS
	Test # 1 Approaches to Problems	___ of 20	
	Test # 2 Problem-Solving Strategies	___ of 30	
	Test # 3 Problems to Solve, Part 1	___ of 35	
	Test # 4 Problems to Solve, Part 2	___ of 30	
	Test # 5 Problem-Solving Process	___ of 25	

TEST DATE	GEOMETRY & MEASUREMENT TESTS	SCORE	COMMENTS & NEEDS
	Test # 1 Plane Geometry	___ of 75	
	Test # 2 Space Geometry	___ of 40	
	Test # 3 Measurement	___ of 90	

TEST DATE	GRAPHING, STATISTICS, & PROBABILITY TESTS	SCORE	COMMENTS & NEEDS
	Test # 1 Coordinate Graphing	___ of 55	
	Test # 2 Probability	___ of 55	
	Test # 3 Statistics & Graphing	___ of 65	

TEST DATE	PRE-ALGEBRA TESTS	SCORE	COMMENTS & NEEDS
	Test # 1 Integers	___ of 50	
	Test # 2 Beginning Equations	___ of 40	
	Test # 3 Equations & Inequalities	___ of 25	

Middle Grade Book of Math Tests

CLASS PROGRESS RECORD — MATH SKILLS
(Numbers & Computation and Fractions & Decimals)

Class _____

Teacher _____

NUMBERS & COMPUTATION TESTS

TEST DATE	TEST	COMMENTS ABOUT RESULTS	SKILLS NEEDING RE-TEACHING
	Test # 1 Whole Number Concepts		
	Test # 2 Addition & Subtraction		
	Test # 3 Multiplication & Division		
	Test # 4 Mixed Operations		

FRACTIONS & DECIMALS TESTS

TEST DATE	TEST	COMMENTS ABOUT RESULTS	SKILLS NEEDING RE-TEACHING
	Test # 1 Fractions		
	Test # 2 Decimals		
	Test # 3 Fractions, Decimals, & Percents		
	Test # 4 Money		

CLASS PROGRESS RECORD — MATH SKILLS

(Problem Solving and Geometry & Measurement)

Class _____

Teacher _____

PROBLEM-SOLVING TESTS

TEST DATE	TEST	COMMENTS ABOUT RESULTS	SKILLS NEEDING RE-TEACHING
	Test # 1 Approaches to Problems		
	Test # 2 Problem-Solving Strategies		
	Test # 3 Problems to Solve, Part 1		
	Test # 4 Problems to Solve, Part 2		
	Test # 5 Problem-Solving Process		

GEOMETRY & MEASUREMENT TESTS

TEST DATE	TEST	COMMENTS ABOUT RESULTS	SKILLS NEEDING RE-TEACHING
	Test # 1 Plane Geometry		
	Test # 2 Space Geometry		
	Test # 3 Measurement		

Middle Grade Book of Math Tests

CLASS PROGRESS RECORD — MATH SKILLS
(Graphing, Statistics, & Probability and Pre-Algebra)

Class _____

Teacher _____

GRAPHING, STATISTICS, & PROBABILITY TESTS

TEST DATE	TEST	COMMENTS ABOUT RESULTS	SKILLS NEEDING RE-TEACHING
	Test # 1 Coordinate Graphing		
	Test # 2 Probability		
	Test # 3 Statistics & Graphing		

PRE-ALGEBRA TESTS

TEST DATE	TEST	COMMENTS ABOUT RESULTS	SKILLS NEEDING RE-TEACHING
	Test # 1 Integers		
	Test # 2 Beginning Equations		
	Test # 3 Equations & Inequalities		

Middle Grade Book of Math Tests

GOOD SKILL SHARPENERS
FOR MATH

The tests in this book will identify student needs for practice, re-teaching or reinforcement of basic skills.

Once those areas of need are known, then what? You and your students need to find some good ways to strengthen those skills.

The BASIC/Not Boring Skills Series, published by Incentive Publications (www.incentivepublications.com), offers 20 books to sharpen basic skills at the Grades 6–8 level. Six of these books are full of math exercises.

The pages of these books are student-friendly, clever, and challenging—guaranteed not to be boring! They cover a wide range of skills, including the skills assessed in this book of tests. A complete checklist of skills is available at the front of each book, complete with a reference list directing you to the precise pages for polishing those skills.

TEST IN THIS BOOK Middle Grade Book of Math Tests	Pages in this Book	You will find pages to sharpen skills in these locations from the BASIC/Not Boring Skills Series, published by Incentive Publications.
Numbers & Computation Test # 1 **Whole Number Concepts & Relationships**	12–17	Gr. 6–8 Whole Numbers & Integers Gr. 6–8 Problem Solving
Numbers & Computation Test # 2 **Addition & Subtraction**	18–21	Gr. 6–8 Whole Numbers & Integers Gr. 6–8 Problem Solving
Numbers & Computation Test # 3 **Multiplication & Division**	22–25	Gr. 6–8 Whole Numbers & Integers Gr. 6–8 Problem Solving
Numbers & Computation Test # 4 **Mixed Operations**	26–31	Gr. 6–8 Whole Numbers & Integers Gr. 6–8 Problem Solving
Fractions & Decimals Test # 1 **Fractions**	34–41	Gr. 6–8 Fractions & Decimals
Fractions & Decimals Test # 2 **Decimals**	42–47	Gr. 6–8 Fractions & Decimals
Fractions & Decimals Test # 3 **Fractions, Decimals, & Percents**	48–51	Gr. 6–8 Fractions & Decimals
Fractions & Decimals Test # 4 **Money**	52–55	Gr. 6–8 Fractions & Decimals Gr. 6–8 Problem Solving

(continued on next page)

(continued on next page)

TEST IN THIS BOOK **Middle Grade Book of Math Tests**	Pages in this Book	You will find pages to sharpen skills in these locations from the BASIC/Not Boring Skills Series, published by Incentive Publications.
Problem-Solving Test # 1 **Approaches to Problems**	58–61	Gr. 6–8 Problem Solving
Problem-Solving Test # 2 **Problem-Solving Strategies**	62–67	Gr. 6–8 Problem Solving
Problem-Solving Tests # 3 and # 4 **Problems to Solve, Part 1** **Problems to Solve, Part 2**	68–73 74–79	Gr. 6–8 Problem Solving Gr. 6–8 Geometry & Measurement Gr. 6–8 Graphing, Statistics, & Probability
Problem-Solving Test # 5 **Problem-Solving Process**	80–83	Gr. 6–8 Problem Solving
Geometry & Measurement Test # 1 **Plane Geometry**	86–93	Gr. 6–8 Geometry & Measurement Gr. 6–8 Problem Solving
Geometry & Measurement Test # 2 **Space Geometry**	94–99	Gr. 6–8 Geometry & Measurement Gr. 6–8 Problem Solving
Geometry & Measurement Test # 3 **Measurement**	100–109	Gr. 6–8 Geometry & Measurement Gr. 6–8 Problem Solving
Graphing, Statistics, & Probability Test # 1 **Coordinate Graphing**	112–117	Gr. 6–8 Graphing, Statistics, & Probability Gr. 6–8 Problem Solving
Graphing, Statistics, & Probability Test # 2 **Probability**	118–123	Gr. 6–8 Graphing, Statistics, & Probability
Graphing, Statistics, & Probability Test # 3 **Statistics & Graphing**	124–133	Gr. 6–8 Graphing, Statistics, & Probability Gr. 6–8 Problem Solving
Pre-Algebra Test # 1 **Integers**	136–141	Gr. 6–8 Pre-Algebra Gr. 6–8 Whole Numbers & Integers
Pre-Algebra Test # 2 **Beginning Equations**	142–147	Gr. 6–8 Pre-Algebra Gr. 6–8 Problem Solving
Pre-Algebra Test # 3 **Equations & Inequalities**	148–152	Gr. 6–8 Pre-Algebra Gr. 6–8 Problem Solving

SCORING GUIDES & ANSWER KEYS

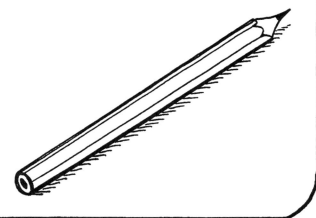

NUMBERS & COMPUTATION TESTS
ANSWER KEY

Whole Number Concepts (Test on page 12)

1. c
2. one hundred fifty-four thousand, eight hundred eighty
3. one hundred eleven thousand, eight
4. seventy-seven million, fifty thousand, fifty
5. 65,400,010
6. 280,104
7. d
8. b
9. 803,450
10. 62,309
11. 90,909
12. 256,369; 256,938; 265,396; 265,398
13. 2, 3, 5, 7, 11, 13, 17, 19, 23, 29
14. millions
15. thousands
16. 0
17. 4
18. 0
19. 55,900
20. 3,625,000
21. 690,000
22. 60,000,000
23. 3300
24. 40,000 + 4000 + 400 + 4
25. $\frac{1}{2}$ of 12,012,000
26. 14, 35, 28, 56, 70
27. 12, 24, 48
28. 1, 2, 3, 6, 9, 18
29. 1, 2, 4
30. 1, 3
31. 6
32. 11
33. 15, 45
34. 7634, 5456
35. 8,200; 7,200

36.

37. <
38. >
39. >
40. <
41. <
42. =
43. >
44. <
45. c
46. d
47. Tallahassee
48. Albuquerque
49. a
50. a & b or b & c

Addition & Subtraction (Test on page 18)

1. d
2. 6
3. Chichi
4. 208
5. 17
6. Lucinda
7. 634,045,135
8. b
9. no
10. 9000
11. 4,993,994
12. 933
13. yes
14. 62, 73, 84
15. 940, 790, 720
16. 157
17. 44,840
18. 20,050,100
19. 888
20. 246,456
21. a
22. 640 hours
23. $705.50
24. 93
25. yes

Middle Grade Book of Math Tests

NUMBERS & COMPUTATION TESTS
ANSWER KEY

Multiplication & Division (Test on page 22)

1. 605 seats
2. 3156 fans
3. 23,275
4. 110
5. 3,809,848
6. 210
7. 160, 32
8. 432; 3888; 11,644
9. a
10. b
11. 13

12. no
13. 16,000
14. 200
15. 5000
16. 100,000
17. 500
18. 90
19. 72,000
20. 40
21. 40,000
22. 22,000

23. e
24. x = 10,290
25. c
26. approx. 15,000 (anything close to this)
27. approx. 250 (anything from 200–300)
28. 3 gal
29. $ .30
30. 5550

Mixed Operations (Test on page 26)

1. multiply
2. divide
3. divide (also accept multiply & divide)
4. c
5. d
6. ÷
7. –
8. x
9. +
10. c
11. a
12. a
13. 772 (accept anything close)
14. b
15. 55,505
16. 33,890
17. 852
18. 409,999
19. 550,000
20. Student should use multiplication to verify the answer.

21. Student should use division to verify the answer.
22. b
23. b
24. A
25. I
26. A
27. D
28. C
29. D
30. C
31. 26
32. 14
33. sprained wrists
34. c
35. b
36. d
37. b
38. no
39. 5
40. 160 miles

Middle Grade Book of Math Tests

FRACTIONS & DECIMALS TESTS ANSWER KEY

Fractions (Test on page 34)

1. $\frac{5}{12}$
2. $67\frac{3}{5}$
3. $12\frac{8}{9}$
4. $86\frac{8}{15}$
5. $11\frac{4}{5}$
6. nine elevenths
7. twenty and three fourths
8. one thousand and one half
9. seven twelfths
10. $\frac{2}{6}$ or $\frac{1}{3}$
11. $\frac{4}{6}$ or $\frac{2}{3}$
12. $\frac{3}{12}$ or $\frac{1}{4}$
13. $\frac{1}{6}$
14. $\frac{3}{6}$ or $\frac{1}{2}$
15. $\frac{2}{3}$
16. $\frac{0}{1}$ or 0

17. $\frac{7}{8}$
18. $\frac{1}{15}$
19. Sal
20. $\frac{1}{21}; \frac{1}{6}; \frac{2}{5}; \frac{5}{8}; \frac{3}{4}; \frac{9}{10}$
21. $\frac{6}{11}; \frac{4}{5}; \frac{2}{3}; \frac{9}{13}$
22. $\frac{5}{16}; \frac{28}{39}; \frac{5}{12}; \frac{11}{18}$
23. $\frac{3}{4}$
24. $\frac{5}{8}$
25. $\frac{4}{5}$
26. $\frac{1}{4}$
27. $\frac{9}{27}; \frac{11}{33}; \frac{4}{12}$
28. $\frac{18}{45}; \frac{2}{5}; \frac{12}{30}$
29. Answers will vary; some possibilities are: $\frac{6}{10}, \frac{9}{15}, \frac{12}{20}, \frac{15}{0}$
30. c
31. $4\frac{3}{5}$

32. $\frac{69}{7}$
33. $6\frac{6}{7}$
34. $18\frac{5}{6}$
35. $\frac{83}{4}$
36. $\frac{11}{12}$
37. $\frac{7}{9}$
38. no
39. $1\frac{1}{3}$
40. $\frac{9}{20}$
41. a
42. e
43. 72
44. d
45. $\frac{5}{9}$
46. $1\frac{1}{15}$
47. c
48. $1\frac{1}{2}$ pizzas
49. $8\frac{9}{11}$

50. yes
51. x = $125\frac{2}{4}$ or $125\frac{1}{2}$
52. y = 66
53. $\frac{6}{13}$
54. 15
55. 7.2 or $7\frac{2}{10}$ minutes
56. .085 quarts
57. 9 minutes
58. 27
59. 8
60. 550
61. 27
62. 14 minutes
63. 2400 meters
64. 126 min or 2 hours, 6 min
65. 75

Decimals (Test on page 42)

1. 9.0009
2. 0.09
3. 9.09
4. 0.909
5. 0.99
6. 0.008
7. 16.9
8. 6.05
9. 8.002
10. twelve and six hundredths
11. seven thousandths
12. one and seventy-seven thousandths
13. 3
14. 6
15. 5
16. 3

17. a. Sly
    b. Bess
    c. Sal
    d. Leroy
    e. Chichi
    f. Spike
18. d
19. 100.8
20. 2.198
21. 4.17
22. 12.0606
23. b
24. 0.9 qt
25. 10.76 mi
26. 1893.946
27. 700.989
28. Sam, 9.014 seconds
29. b

30. 20,021.1
31–36. Problems solved correctly are: 33, 34, 36
37. 0.39
38. no
39. x = 0.07
40. y = 60.25
41. 89.7%
42. 89.907%
43. 8.97%
44. 8907%
45. 0.89077%
46. 8.79%
47. 173.52 hours
48. 176 cm
49. 11
50. 18.1°

Middle Grade Book of Math Tests   Copyright ©2001 by Incentive Publications, Inc., Nashville, TN.

FRACTIONS & DECIMALS TESTS ANSWER KEY

Fractions, Decimals, & Percents (Test on page 48)

1. 0.86
2. 0.6
3. 0.67
4. $\frac{8}{10}$ or $\frac{4}{5}$
5. $\frac{15}{100}$ or $\frac{3}{20}$
6. $4\frac{16}{100}$ or $4\frac{4}{25}$
7. a
8. d
9. 0.0603
10. 0.485
11. 0.127
12. 1.4005
13. 3004%
14. 96%
15. 0.49%

16. 3702.7%
17. 6.9
18. 0.069
19. 0.0069
20. 0.69
21. 0.00069
22. 0.0609
23. 33
24. b
25. 1500
26. 2225
27. 4%
28. B, E
29. 60%
30. $\frac{7}{100}$

31. 47.11
32. 0.8; 80%
33. $\frac{9}{100}$; 9%
34. $\frac{1}{3}$; 0.333
35. 0.4; 40%
36. $\frac{3}{4}$; 75%
37. $1\frac{6}{10}$; 160%
38. $\frac{2}{100}$; 0.02
39. 0.20; 20%
40. 21.841 lb. or 21.84 lb.
41. 1620 ft
42. 6250 ft
43. 15 qts
44. $\frac{9}{25}$ or 36% or 0.36
45. A. 75%
    B. 9 pounds

Money (Test on page 52)

1. $705
2. $540
3. Buster
4. Roxie
5. Spike
6. $575
7. Rhoda
8. 1
9. $723.65

10. $10,088.82
11. $10.50
12. $16.25
13. b
14. a
15. no
16. no
17. $100,600
18. $490,000

19. Equations may vary:
    Answer: x = $50,000
20. x = $182,000.50
21. Use division to verify answer
22. $30.76
23. 4050
24. $1200–$1800
25. $9706.00

Middle Grade Book of Math Tests

PROBLEM-SOLVING TESTS ANSWER KEY

Approaches to Problems (Test on page 58)

1–5. The following problems should have an X: 3, 5
6. Draw a line through:
38% of them were bought at the Sky Thrills Shop.

50% of the chutes have red and white stripes on the canopy.
7. b, d
8. a, d
9. b, c
10. Missing information is: the number of cars
11. x, +
12. ÷, −
13. multiplication or multiplication and division
14. multiplication
15. subtraction
16. multiplication, addition, & subtraction
17–20: Student answers may vary somewhat from these. Allow any order of operations that the student can explain.
17. a
18. c
19. a
20. c

Problem-Solving Strategies (Test on page 62)

1–3: Equations may vary somewhat. Elements may appear in several different orders in an equation. One or two possibilities are given for each. (Student may use any letter other than x for the variable.)

1. Equation:
$$44n = 132$$
$$n \times 44 = 132$$
$$n = 132 \div 44$$
Answer: 3 boats

2. Equation:
$$x + 19 + 12 + 17 = 148$$
$$148 - 19 - 12 - 17 = x$$
Answer: 100

3. Equation:
$$6x + 18 = 258$$
$$258 - 18 = 6x$$
Answer: $40

4. 220, 145, 110
5. 0, −1100
6. 5% better than Week # 3. OR 5.4 mph (answer may be approximate)
7. 2900 m
8. 4500 yd^2
9. 1.19 mi^2
10. 3410 ft^3
11. 2197 cm^3
12. 79,128 cm^3
13. A. 210 ft
    B. 2450 ft^2
    C. 49,000 ft^3
14. answers will vary; approx. 240–300 hours
15. answers will vary; approx. $120
16. D
17. 89 lbs
18. 1:40 A.M. (Friday)
19. no
20. Spike: 8, Coach: 40
21. 432
22–23: Proportions may vary. Check to see that they make sense for the problem.
22. Proportion $\frac{3}{16} = \frac{x}{240}$
    Answer: 45
23. Proportion $\frac{5}{12} = \frac{70}{x}$
    Answer: 168
24. 4 hours, 18$\frac{1}{2}$ minutes (students may also give answer in seconds)
25–30: The answers given are the strategies most likely to be used. If a student chooses a different strategy, ask for a demonstration of how he or she would use that strategy to solve the problem.
25. g
26. b or e
27. d or g
28. a, d, or g
29. f
30. a

Middle Grade Book of Math Tests

PROBLEM-SOLVING TESTS ANSWER KEY

Problems to Solve, Part 1 (Test on page 68)

1–5. Equations may vary somewhat. There are several different orders that elements may appear in an equation. One possibility is given for each. (Student may use any letter for the variable.)

1. Equation:
$$13 + 28 - x = 7$$
Answer: $x = 34$

2. Equation:
$$x + 6\frac{1}{2} = 12\frac{5}{8}$$
Answer: $x = 6\frac{1}{8}$

3. Equation:
$$0.33 + x = 3.3 + 3.66$$
Answer: $x = 6.63$

4. Equation:
$$400 - x = 87.5$$
Answer: $x = 312.5$

5. Equation:
$$12 \times 250 = x + 2700$$
Answer: $x = 300$

6. 770
7. 185
8. 4608
9. 280
10. $12\frac{1}{2}$
11. $5250
12. sweatshirt & t-shirt
13. no
14. $229
15. $21
16. bumper sticker
17. Houndsville
18. Canine City
19. Wooferville
20. Dogs' Corners
21. 478.8 liters
22. 3.35 min
23. 4:05 P.M.
24. 11:45 P.M.
25. Monday, 4:43 A.M.
26. 37, 19
27. There are many possible combinations. Here are two: 16 dimes and 5 nickels; 6 quarters, 10 pennies, and 5 nickels
28. Here are some possibilities: 3 and 36; 4 and 27; 6 and 18; 9 and 12
29. 25
30. 18
31. 120
32. 1044 miles
33. $228
34. 5
35. C

Problems to Solve, Part 2 (Test on page 74)

1. tent
2. $194.57 or $194.56
3. $155.93 or $155.92
4. $258.83 or $258.82
5. 7.22 m (or 7.2 or 7.222)
6. 4.14 m^2
7. 247 in
8. 2150 m
9. 8750 m^2
10. 157,500 m^3
11. Josie
12. Dixie
13. Chichi
14. about 215 (allow any answer that is close)
15. Leroy
16. B
17. d
18. $\frac{20}{48}$ or $\frac{5}{12}$
19. $\frac{12}{48}$ or $\frac{1}{4}$
20. $\frac{16}{48}$ or $\frac{1}{3}$
21. $\frac{28}{48}$ or $\frac{7}{12}$
22. Spike & Roxie, Spike & Rufus, Spike & Leroy, Spike & Dixie, Spike & Chichi, Roxie & Rufus, Roxie & Leroy, Roxie & Dixie, Roxie & Chichi, Rufus & Leroy, Rufus & Dixie, Rufus & Chichi, Leroy & Dixie, Leroy & Chichi, Dixie & Chichi
23. b
24. c
25. 15
26. d
27. Wrong: Correct answer is 14,622 ft
28. Correct
29. Correct
30. Wrong: Correct answer is 60 hrs & 15 min

Problem-Solving Process (Test on page 80)

Use the scoring guide found on page 168 to give students scores for this test.

Problem # 1—34 in
Problem # 2—Sly
Problem # 3—$405.78
Problem # 4—180
Problem # 5—23 and 32
Problem # 6—Tuesday, 3:22 a.m.
Problem # 7—29 cans

Middle Grade Book of Math Tests

PROBLEM SOLVING PROCESS SCORING GUIDE

TRAIT	SCORE OF 5	SCORE OF 3	SCORE OF 1
CONCEPTUAL UNDERSTANDING	• Student's work shows that the problem is clearly identified and understood. • Work clearly shows that the student has translated the written problem-solving task effectively into mathematical ideas.	• Student's work shows that the problem is identified and understood. • The student has done an adequate job of translating the written problem-solving task into mathematical ideas.	• Student's work does not show a clear identification or understanding of the problem. • The student has done a partial or incorrect job of translating the written problem-solving task into mathematical ideas.
STRATEGIES & PROCESSES	• Student has chosen appropriate strategies for solving the problem. • The strategies have been used in a complete, clear, and complex manner to move toward a problem solution. • Equations, symbols, models, pictures, and/or diagrams are clear and complete.	• Student has chosen appropriate strategies for solving the problem. • The strategies have been used in a complete, clear, and complex manner to move toward a problem solution. • Equations, symbols, models, pictures, and/or diagrams are complete and relatively clear.	• Student has not chosen appropriate strategies for solving the problem or has chosen appropriate strategies but not used them correctly or effectively. • Equations, symbols, models, pictures and/or diagrams are incomplete or do not lead to the solution.
COMMUNICATION	• The student has used words, symbols, pictures, models, and/or other graphics to clearly show the steps to a solution of the problem. • The student's explanation of the use of strategies and of the path taken to solution is clear and sensible.	• The student has used words, symbols, pictures, models, and/or other graphics to adequately show the steps to a solution of the problem. • The student's explanation of the use of strategies and of the path taken to solution is adequate.	• The student has not adequately used words, symbols, pictures, models, and/or other graphics to clearly show the steps to a solution of the problem. • The communication of the student's processes is skimpy, or nonexistent.
CORRECTNESS (Accuracy of the Answer)	• The student's answer is correct. • The student's work supports the answer given.	• The student's answer is mostly correct, with only minor errors. • The student's work supports the answer.	• The student's answer is incomplete, or incorrect. *and/or* • The student's work does not support the answer given.
VERIFICATION	• The student's work shows that he/she has reviewed the problem-solving process and made a clear, effective attempt to justify the answer or arrive at it in a different way. • The review supports the student's solution.	• The student's work shows that he/she has reviewed the problem-solving process and made an attempt to justify the answer. • The review supports the student's solution.	• The student's work does not show an effective or complete review of his/her process, or a defense or support of his/her solution.

A score of 4 may be given for papers that fall between 3 and 5 on a trait. A score of 2 may be given for papers that fall between 1 and 3.

Middle Grade Book of Math Tests

GEOMETRY & MEASUREMENT TESTS
ANSWER KEY

Plane Geometry (Test on page 86)

1. b
2. b, c, d
3. d
4. b
5. b
6. a
7. b
8. c, d, e
9. b, c
10. C
11. A
12. B
13. A
14. E, G, I
15. B, C, D, F, J, K
16. D & E, J & G, or K & I
17. B and C
18. K and J or G and I
19. d
20. b

21. B
22. CD
23. EF or GH or CD
24. AC, AD, AB
25. CAB or DAB or BAC or BAD
26. no
27. 3, 4, 2
28. 5
29. 3
30. 1
31. F
32. F
33. T
34. F
35. T
36. A, G
37. I
38. A, B, C, G, J
39. H
40. E
41. A, B, C, G

42. b
43. e
44. b
45. T
46. T
47. F
48. T
49. T
50. F
51. F
52. B, C, E, G
53. yes
54. yes
55. no
56. yes
57. a
58. d
59. 420 ft
60. 8400 ft^2
61. 63 in
62. 180 in^2
63. 62.8 cm

64. 314 cm^2
65. 400 m
66. 9500 m^2
67. 32 yd
68. 64 yd^2
69. 850 cm
70. 27,500 cm^2
71. b
72. A. flip
   B. slide
   C. turn (or slide)
73. Check to see that student has drawn a turn of the figure.
74. Check to see that student has drawn a flip of the figure.
75. Check to see that student has drawn a slide of the figure.

Space Geometry (Test on page 94)

1. cube
2. triangular prism
3. rectangular prism
4. hexagonal prism
5. cylinder
6. pyramid
7. cone
8. sphere
9. cube
10. cone
11. cylinder
12. sphere
13. pyramid
14. rectangular prism (or cube)
15. triangular prism
16. pentagonal prism

17. 12
18. 0
19. 9
20. 5
21. $V = s^3$
22. $V = \frac{4}{3}\pi r^3$
23. $V = \frac{1}{3}Bh$
24. $V = \pi r^2 h$
25. $V = \frac{1}{3}\pi r^2 h$
26. $V = Bh$
27. $V = Bh$
28. cylinder
29. 706.5 in^2
30. 7065 in^3

31. Formula: $V = s^3$
   $V = 512$ m^3
32. Formula: $V = \frac{1}{3}Bh$
   $V = 1200$ m^3
33. Formula: $V = Bh$
   $V = 1500$ in^3
34. Formula: $V = Bh$
   $V = 126$ ft^3
35. approx 79.5 in^3 or 79.6 in^3
36. approx 60 in^3
37. Leroy
38. approx. 119.05 in^3
39. A. dome tent
   B. dome tent
40. C

Middle Grade Book of Math Tests

GEOMETRY & MEASUREMENT TESTS
ANSWER KEY

Measurement (Test on page 100)

1. weight
2. capacity
3. capacity
4. length
5. time
6. length
7. weight
8. length
9. length
10. length
11. capacity
12. length
13. capacity
14. weight
15. capacity
16. length
17. capacity
18. temperature
19. time
20. length
21. e
22. d
23. b
24. >
25. >
26. <
27. <
28. <
29. <
30. =
31. =

32. c
33. b
34. c
35. a
36. c
37. d
38. d
39. a
40. d or c
41. b
42. c
43. c
44. a
45. 2
46. 3000
47. 5
48. 1.5
49. 70
50. 450
51. 120
52. 60
53. 141
54. 21, 120
55. 68
56. 2
57. 80
58. 780
59. 49
60. 216
61. $2\frac{1}{2}$ in
62. 8 cm

63. 14 cm
64. 9 in or 10 in
65. 300 m
66. 250 m
67. c
68. b
69. c
70. d
71. 11 cm^2
72. 1.5 in^2
73. 570 ft^2
74. 50.24 m^2
75. 3 in^3
76. 167.47 in^3
77. 96 in^3
78. 12,560 cm^3
79. 360,000 liters
80. no
81. 10 in.
82. d
83. c
84. 9:30
85. 5:20
86. A. 3
    B. 2
    C. 1
87. 15 miles
88. 3000 g or 3 kg
89. 77 min
90. 54 cups

Middle Grade Book of Math Tests

GRAPHING, STATISTICS, & PROBABILITY TESTS ANSWER KEY

Coordinate Graphing (Test on page 112)

1. bike
2. mitt
3. skate
4. ball (beachball or baseball)
5. soccer ball
6. (–7, 0)
7. (0, 4)
8. (2, 0)
9. (–4, 6)
10. (6, 8)
11. (–6, 11)
12. (0, 9)
13. (6, 0)
14. (–5, 6)
15. (–3, 0)
16. (4, 5)
17. (7, 8)
18–24. Check student graphs to see that darts are drawn in correct locations.

25. B
26. A
27. M
28. P
29. (–5, –5)
30. (3, –6)
31. (3, 3)
32. (–7, 3)
33. (–5, 6)
34–43. Check student graphs to see that stars and comet are drawn in correct locations.

44–53:

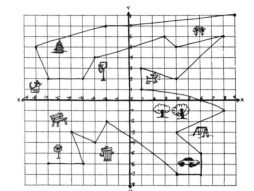

54–55.

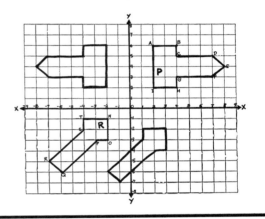

Probability (Test on page 118)

1. 2
2. 6
3. 4
4. 3
5. 12
6. 5
7. purple
8. red
9. yellow and blue
10. red
11. HHH, TTT, HHT, HTT, HTH, THT, TTH, THH

12. $\frac{1}{4}$
13. 1
14. $\frac{2}{7}$
15. $\frac{3}{6}$ or $\frac{1}{2}$
16. $\frac{2}{8}$ or $\frac{1}{4}$
17. $\frac{1}{8}$
18. $\frac{3}{8}$
19. $\frac{6}{8}$ or $\frac{3}{4}$
20. $\frac{3}{8}$
21. $\frac{3}{6}$ or $\frac{1}{2}$
22. $\frac{2}{6}$ or $\frac{1}{3}$
23. $\frac{1}{6}$
24. $\frac{2}{6}$ or $\frac{1}{3}$

25. $\frac{5}{6}$
26. $\frac{32}{48}$ or $\frac{2}{3}$
27. $\frac{11}{48}$
28. $\frac{9}{48}$ or $\frac{3}{16}$
29. $\frac{36}{48}$ or $\frac{3}{4}$
30. $\frac{16}{48}$ or $\frac{1}{3}$
31. $\frac{37}{48}$
32. $\frac{11}{34}$
33. $\frac{28}{34}$ or $\frac{14}{17}$
34. $\frac{17}{34}$ or $\frac{1}{2}$
35. $\frac{9}{34}$
36. $\frac{23}{34}$
37. $\frac{14}{34}$ or $\frac{7}{12}$

38. Pairs are: S-B, S-P, S-R, S-L, S-J, B-P, B-R, B-L, B-J, P-R, P-L, P-J, R-L, R-J, L-J
39. m-t, m-f, m-o, m-b, y-t, y-f, y-o, y-b, c-t, c-f, c-o, c-b, r-t, r-f, r-o, r-b
40. 24
41. $\frac{1}{10}$
42. $\frac{4}{10}$ or $\frac{2}{5}$
43. $\frac{2}{10}$ or $\frac{1}{5}$

44. $\frac{1}{10}$
45. $\frac{3}{10}$
46. $\frac{8}{18}$ or $\frac{4}{9}$
47. $\frac{6}{17}$
48. $\frac{5}{51}$
49. $\frac{3}{7}$
50. $\frac{8}{2}$ or $\frac{4}{1}$
51. $\frac{5}{5}$ or 1
52. 80
53. 320
54. $\frac{30}{105}$ or $\frac{6}{21}$
55. 6

Middle Grade Book of Math Tests

GRAPHING, STATISTICS, & PROBABILITY TESTS
ANSWER KEY

Statistics & Graphing (Test on page 124)

1. g
2. a
3. d
4. c
5. e
6. h
7. f
8. b
9. increase
10. 100,000 – 125,000
11. 8
12. a
13. middle school and high school
14. ages 65–75 and over 75
15. 3
16. ages 26–40
17. b
18. 11.9 min
19. 4.5–25 min
20. 11.5
21. 8 hours, 24 min

22. 4 hours, 42 min
23. 3–26
24. 8
25. 4
26. 9–16
27. 9
28. 9
29. 2–32
30. 11
31. 12
32. 2–52
33. 6.5
34. 2
35. 45
36. 30
37. Game 1
38. 37
39. 43
40. Spike, J.J.
41. school groups
42. tour groups
43. families

44. 3000
45. 300
46. 5700
47. M-T-W
48. c
49. 18 or 19
50. Saturday
51. a
52. bungee jumping
53. approx 1800
54. kayaking
55. 2200
56. 1300
57. 4
58. Down Home Grille
59. $200,000
60. Casa Grande
61. b
62. d
63. a
64. Mexican
65. b

PRE-ALGEBRA TESTS ANSWER KEY

Integers (Test on page 136)

1. −9
2. 29
3. 30
4. 0.05
5. $-6\frac{1}{2}$
6. 24.5
7. 113
8. $\frac{12}{7}$
9. >
10. >
11. >
12. >
13. <
14. >
15. −25, −18.6, −3, 3, 12, 18.6, 25
16. −90.5 ft
17. 86
18. 36
19. −77
20. 47.8 m
21. 7
22. −74
23. −40
24. −$185
25. −3.7° F
26. −3333
27. −104
28. −100
29. 24
30. −33
31. 100,000
32. b
33. a
34. c
35. b
36. Student should use multiplication to verify answer or complete the division work.
37. b
38. a, d
39. 10
40. −50
41. 14,700
42. 56,000
43. c
44. d
45. c
46. b
47. −80 ft
48. −46.5° or 80.5°
49. −5.3°
50. 12

Beginning Equations (Test on page 142)

1. 11
2. 11 and 38
3. b
4. c
5. 2(h + u); may vary somewhat.
6. s − e
7. p ÷ n or $\frac{p}{n}$
8. d
9. 64b
10. 5n
11. 4p + 2
12. 19k + 12
13. 4a + 45d
14. 4z + 1
15. C
16. I
17. D
18. A
19. Z
20. a
21. c
22. c
23. b
24–25. Equations may vary somewhat.
24. $a = \frac{1}{3}m$
25. a = w + $30
26. b
27. a
28. d; answer: 42
29. b; answer: 21 qt
30. c; answer: 77 min
31.   2 x = 78 *OR*
         2x + 6 = 84
32.   18p = 72 *OR*
         18p + 48 = 120
33.   6x = −45 *OR*
         6x + 5 = −40
34.   2n = 60 *OR*
         710 + 2n = 770
35. n = 6200
36. x = 5
37. n = 10
38. x = 55
39. Bud is 16; Wally is 12
40. Al is 8; Ed is 3

Middle Grade Book of Math Tests

PRE-ALGEBRA TESTS ANSWER KEY

Equations & Inequalities (Test on page 148)

1. x = 4
2. x = 70
3. x = 356
4. x = −364
5. x = 8
6. x = −14
7. yes
8. yes
9. c; x = $9\frac{1}{4}$
10. a; x = 5

11–14: Equations may vary somewhat.

11. Equation: x + (x − 9) = 47
    Solution: x = 28

12. Equation: $\frac{288}{4.5}$ = x
    OR   288 ÷ 4.5 = x
    OR   4.5x = 288
    Solution: x = 64 mph

13. Equation: x + 67 = 58
    Solution: x = −9° F

14. Equation: $\frac{12 + 10 + 14 + x}{4}$ = 11
    OR   (12 + 10 + 14 + x) ÷ 4 = 11
    Solution: x = 8 hours

15. −3, 5
16. 3, 7
17. −30, 4, 15, −9
18. 2, −12, −10
19. a
20. b
21. A. 9
    B. 5

22.   x = −2;   y = 12
     x = 7;   y = −15
     x = 4;   y = −6
     x = 10;   y = 36

23.   y = 20;   x = −5
     y = −40;   x = 10
     y = 24;   x = −6
     y = −16;   x = 4

24. c
25. a